In this explosively frank collectio  Adriana X. Jacobs, Vaan Nguyen t textures and terrains of intimate s₁ ...overs and ex-lovers, travelers in lands both foreign and familiar, the individual self alone with a mind that can't help but see the world through interstices. Here is a visionary moving along the edge of reality and its surreal offerings: where the flora and fauna of a natural world intersect with the tensions of women and men. "Look at me, I'm a routine," Nguyen writes, and she's right, though the truth is tongue-in-cheek: Nguyen's lyrical routine is nothing short of exquisite, full of verve, full of nails.

—Diana Khoi Nguyen, *Ghost Of* (Omnidawn)

Vaan Nguyen's electric poems of lust, longing, and detachment are both quintessentially Tel Aviv and entirely her own. Elegantly introduced and translated by Adriana X. Jacobs, this collection offers the English-language reader an essential window into the true and often surprisingly multilingual and multiethnic diversity of contemporary Israeli poetry—as it brings Nguyen's linguistic journey from her family's native Vietnamese to her native Hebrew all the way to the shores of English.

—Aviya Kushner, *The Grammar of God* (Spiegel & Grau) and *Wolf Lamb Bomb* (Orison Books)

The Truffle Eye
עין הכמהין

Vaan Nguyen
ואן נוייֵן

Translated from Hebrew by
Adriana X. Jacobs

Zephyr Press | Brookline, Mass.

Hebrew Copyright © 2021 by Thi Hong Van Nguyen
English Translation and Foreword Copyright © 2021 by Adriana X. Jacobs
Cover art: from the series *The Atlas* by Lihi Turjeman
All rights reserved.
Book and cover design by *type*slowly

Printed in Michigan by Cushing Malloy, Inc.

This publication is made possible in part by the Academy of American Poets
with funds from the Amazon Literary Partnership Poetry Fund.

Zephyr Press acknowledges with gratitude the financial
support of the Massachusetts Cultural Council
and the National Endowment for the Arts.

Zephyr Press, a non-profit arts and education 501(c)(3) organization,
publishes literary titles that foster a deeper understanding of cultures
and languages. Zephyr Press books are distributed worldwide
by Consortium Book Sales and Distribution [www.cbsd.com].

Cataloguing-in publication data is available from the Library of Congress.

ISBN 978-1938890-82-6

ZEPHYR PRESS
www.zephyrpress.org

Table of Contents

Translating Roots:
Introducing the Poetry of Vaan Nguyen

No one flinches when I mention that I am translating an Israeli poet with a Hebrew, Russian, Spanish or English-sounding name. The name "Vaan Nguyen," on the other hand, has elicited incredulity more times than I can count over the past decade. This reaction says something not only about perceptions of Israeli literature, but also about the great need for translations to reflect the diversity of ethnicities and languages that constitute Israeli culture. In the process of bringing Nguyen's Hebrew poetry to Anglophone readers, I have wrestled with the question of how to present her and her work, given the attention that her cultural background brings. Nguyen's poetry circulates as part of a rich Vietnamese literary diaspora that includes Vietnamese American writers like Ocean Vuong, Viet Thanh Nguyen, and Monique Truong. And yet, introducing Nguyen's poetry to the Anglophone reader needs to account for the particularities of the Vietnamese experience in Israel, without letting this history overshadow her work. Since this history remains largely unfamiliar to readers outside of Israel, I'll begin there.

In June 1977, an Israeli freighter, the *Yuvali*, came across a boat of Vietnamese refugees drifting in the South China Sea. Bordering countries refused the passengers entry until Israel agreed to offer them asylum and resettlement, Menachem Begin's first act as Israel's newly elected Prime Minister. At that point, the passengers were allowed to disembark in Taiwan and make their way to Israel, where the saga of the Boat People, as they were known, prompted comparisons to the plight of

Jewish refugees in World War II. For Prime Minister Begin, this humanitarian gesture was also politically calculated. His party, Likud, had scored a historic electoral win over the Labor Party (Ha-ʿavoda), which had dominated Israeli politics since the establishment of the State. The story goes that Begin was hoping that his magnanimous gesture would help ameliorate international concerns over this major political "realignment," as it came to be known. Between 1977 and 1979, approximately 360 Vietnamese refugees entered Israel in three waves and, of that number, about half left for the United States or Europe. Those who stayed were able to attain Israeli citizenship, take on jobs, start families, and continue their lives.[1] Though as Evyn Lê Espiritu Gandhi has noted, "the refugee condition—un-belonging in the nation-state—does not disappear after the singular event of parental absorption."[2]

Nguyen's parents were among the third wave of refugees who came in 1979. She was born in Ashkelon, Israel in 1982, one of five daughters. The family moved around and eventually settled in Jaffa Dalet, a working-class—largely immigrant and Arab—neighborhood that is part of the Tel Aviv-Jaffa municipality, "not the pastoral tourist part, but the section that is far from the sea," Nguyen explains.[3]

1. Part of this introduction draws from work that I previously published. See Adriana X. Jacobs, "Releasing Roots: On Translating Vaan Nguyen," *PEN/America* (October 2. 2015) and "Where You Are From: The Poetry of Vaan Nguyen." *Shofar: An Interdisciplinary Journal of Jewish Studies 33.4, Contemporary Israeli Literature* (2015): 83–110.

2. Evyn Lê Espiritu, "Vexed Solidarities: Vietnamese Israelis and the Question of Palestine," *Lit: Literature Interpretation Theory*, 29:1 (2018): 19.

3. Coby Ben-Simhon, "In Her Words," *Haaretz*, March 27, 2008 (English).

Her connection to this history is understandably complicated. In her words, "Whenever a humanitarian crisis pops up, I'm approached by various media outlets that want to interview me about the refugee experience, but the only thing I can do is read poetry at one of *Maayan*'s flash readings, because I am a poet who does not feel like a refugee."[4] Although her parents spoke Vietnamese at home, Nguyen feels most at home in her native Hebrew.

This is apparent in Duki Dror's 2005 documentary *The Journey of Vaan Nguyen*, which follows Nguyen and her father Hoài Mỹ Nguyễn on a trip back to Vietnam to attempt to reclaim land taken from her family during the communist takeover of the country. At the end of the film, we follow Nguyen as she walks through Hanoi, acknowledging, in Hebrew, "I am here as a tourist, as an Israeli."[5] But poems like "Jaffa D" touch on the complex language politics of Israel/Palestine. The lines "the slave torn from language / enters the jail" recall how Vietnamese refugees were required to learn Hebrew as part of the process of cultural absorption that Jewish immigrants undergo. And more broadly, it gestures to the hegemony of Hebrew, which eclipses major local languages like Arabic and Russian, as well as the other languages that immigrants carry with them.

A few years ago, after a reading at the University of Cambridge, Nguyen was asked how she became a poet. She delivered a characteristically tongue-in-cheek response, relating how, in the early 2000s, a reader of her blog told her that she could turn her posts into poems with some extra line breaks. "And that's how I became

4. Vaan Nguyen, "The Boat People—The Next Generation?" *Ynet*, September 8, 2015 (Hebrew).

5. Duki Dror, dir. *The Journey of Vaan Nguyen* (2005, Zygote Films).

a poet." This account doesn't tell the whole story, but it isn't entirely off the mark. Nguyen's blog had caught the eye of poet and editor Roy "Chicky" Arad who published her first poems in 2005, in the second issue of his then-fledgling journal *Maayan* (Source). From there, Nguyen's poems made their way to Israel's mainstream daily newspapers, including *Maariv* and *Haaretz*, which remain vital public platforms for poets in Israel today. Her 2008 chapbook *Eyn ha-kemihin* (The Truffle Eye) was widely reviewed and brought her increased public attention. An expanded book edition followed in 2013, also published by Maayan Press. But Nguyen's statement highlights how she has charted her own path in Israeli Hebrew letters against the cliques, power dynamics, and market pressures that consign many other writers to anonymity. In an early interview, Nguyen acknowledged *Maayan's* commitment to bringing attention to the peripheries of Israel's literary culture. In so doing, the journal provided a critical support network that helped her "breach that anonymity," while also freeing her to forge her own relations both within and outside of the Israeli poetry scene.[6]

When *The Truffle Eye* first appeared in 2008, many reviews highlighted Nguyen's cultural background as evidence of the widening field of Israeli literature, but a number of critics also made it a point to mark her work as different and exotic. Nguyen confronts these expectations from the onset, opening her collection with the poem "Mekong River":

הַלַּיְלָה חָלַפְתִּי עַל שָׁלוֹשׁ מִטּוֹת
כְּמוֹ שַׁטְתִּי בַּמֶּקוֹנְג
וְלָחַשְׁתִּי אֶת יְפִי הַפְּרָת הַחִדֶּקֶל.

---

6. Ben-Simhon, "In Her Words."

Tonight I moved between three beds
like I was sailing on the Mekong
and whispered the beauty of the Tigris and the Euphrates.

At first glance, the poem's reference to the Mekong River appears to settle any questions of affiliation and location. We expect that this poem, like others in this collection, will address cultural identity and specifically Nguyen's Vietnamese heritage. Except that Nguyen introduces a simile that unsettles any expectation of a straightforward relation to Vietnam. For what does it mean to move "like" one is sailing on the Mekong River? Similes create relations but they also acknowledge a degree of distance and difference. Is the speaker near this river or far away? The Mekong is a transboundary river that runs through China, Myanmar, Laos, Thailand, Cambodia, and Vietnam; in Nguyen's cartography it also intersects with the Tigris-Euphrates river system, which runs through present day Syria, Iraq, Iran, Turkey, and Kuwait. Israeli readers, however, are likely to discern here a reference to Chaim Nachman Bialik's "Between the Tigris and Euphrates," an early twentieth century Hebrew poem that was later set to music (including a popular version by the late Mizrahi singer Ofra Haza). These rivers may not flow through Israel, but in this intertextual moment, they come into contact as part of Nguyen's personal poetic map, one which includes coordinates for Hanoi, Tel Aviv-Jaffa, New York City, Herzliya, Tyrol, Paris, Milan, Salzburg, Pasadena, and more. Add to this the "three beds" that open the poem, indications of the everyday migrations we make between lovers, work, school, home. The last line of the poem—"who dares abandon a disease mid-sea?"—places these movements in a more explicit relation with the history of

Vietnamese refugees in Israel, but even here, Nguyen's coordinates remain fluid, connecting her "mid-sea" to the other seas of Hebrew literature. From the Book of Jonah to contemporary Israeli poetry, the Hebrew *yam*—sea—is a space of voyage and discovery, loss and transformation, not to mention a radical alternative to settlement and territory.

In Hebrew, the words for truffle—*kemihin*—and longing—*kemiha*—appear to share a root, a detail underscored in the Talmud tractate Genesis Rabba 69:1, where we find the following exposition:

> R. Yosi b. Zimra began his discourse, 'My flesh longs (*kamah*) for you in a dry and weary land without water.' [Psalm 63:2] R. El'azar, in the name of R. Yosi b. Zimra [said,] 'My soul thirsts for you, [my flesh] longs for you.' R. Aibo said, 'Like mushrooms (*kemehot*) that hope for water.'[7]

It is not clear from Rav Aibo's *mashal* (proverb) just how versed he was in truffle ecology, but truffles were known to ancient writers, some of whom theorized that they required thunder and lightning to grow. Indeed, even today Bedouin truffle hunters seek out the desert truffle—*Terfezia leonis* or *kemeha*, in Hebrew—where lightning strikes during the November-December rain season. Their appearance, like the European varieties, is nonetheless unpredictable, making them a rare and highly sought-after delicacy. It takes years and the right conditions for the intricate, subterranean network (mycelium) that makes them possible to form. This network is mycorrhizal,

---

7. I have taken this translation from Benjamin Williams, *Commentary on Midrash Rabba in the Sixteenth Century: The* Or ha-Sekhel *of Abraham ben Asher* (Oxford: Oxford UP, 2016): 115.

in a symbiotic relationship with different varieties of trees and plants which can come to rely on the nutrients the truffle fungi provide. The complexity of this system has challenged attempts to cultivate, not to mention domesticate, the truffle; therefore, by invoking the truffle as the opening image of her poetry collection, Nguyen is arguably projecting this resistance and difficulty to her own poems.

Rav Aibo's simile draws a relation between truffles and longing that I also see at work in Nguyen's title story, "The Truffle Eye," which begins with a startling transformation: a man wakes up one morning to find that he has become a woman with truffle eyes. Curiously, this does not appear to trouble her co-workers, who carry on in their interactions with her as if nothing has changed. But the truffle eyes catch the attention of a group of men who follow her home and who insist that she hand them over. (The Hebrew spelling of her name, Eva, links it to the root for "desire.") It's not a stretch to read this story as Nguyen's critique of her own reception, as an address to readers and critics who were quick to label her work as "exotic," while hailing it as a validation of Israeli multiculturalism. In this context, it is telling that the cover of her chapbook featured a close-up of Nguyen's face, drawing us to her eyes, which are directed to the left of our gaze. Since Hebrew is a right-to-left language, this composition suggests that Nguyen is moving us away from her face and into the poems themselves. Here it may be helpful to point out that the Hebrew *ayin*—eye—also means "source" or "fountain," from which we get *ma'ayan*, the name of the journal and press that published her early poems.

Reading Nguyen's poetry can feel like you're playing with the zoom feature on your phone camera. For instance, a poem that begins with a man missing his train ends several lines later on a New

York City rooftop ("On the Hudson"). In another, we move from an indoor pool "in the Pyrenees" to a "stairwell in Tel Aviv" bracing for a rocket strike. I was drawn to translating Nguyen's poetry because of these movements, but also because she resists connecting these coordinates. In "Culture Stain," the speaker is asked "where are you from?" but refuses to give a straight answer. Or rather, her answer, "I come from this rot," is not what her interlocutor expects ("I mean, parents?"). But immigrant pasts—not to mention languages—are tenacious, as the poet Avot Yeshurun observed when he wrote "I walked in you in the town I left" (trans. Harold Schimmel). Nguyen was born in Israel, but her work explores, as many Hebrew poets before her have done, the tension between the "culture stains" we inherit and our desire to strike our own roots in the world.

Translating Nguyen's poetry, and this book in particular, gave me the opportunity to consider the movements that have textured my own life. In college, I was a student of Latin American literature. My first major translation project was a translation into English of the poetry of *Los decapitados*, a group of Ecuadorian Modernists. Then one weekend, during my junior year abroad in Chile, I met a pair of Israelis on a camping trip, heard Hebrew spoken for the first time, and redirected the course of my life. I began to study Hebrew, then went to Israel for a year (which became three) and returned to the United States to write a dissertation on modern Hebrew poetry. How did I get there? Maybe it started on July 20, 1969, the day of the Apollo lunar landing, which is also the day that my Ecuadorian mother landed in Chicago, the first day of a vacation that stretched to fifty years. But if we go there, we also could go to my Scottish ancestor, who crossed the Atlantic and joined George Washington's regiment. Or the Italian great-great-great-grandmother who ended up in Peru for reasons that we will never fully know. But as "Culture Stain" acknowledges, genealogies can be too straightforward, and even selective, as answers to the question "where are you from?" The stories of our lives go through numerous retellings and reinventions as we move across seas, borders, languages, "three beds."

What also drew me to Nguyen's work is that it takes Hebrew out of its linguistic, cultural, and even political comfort zones. I wanted the English translations to do that too, but it meant unsettling my own English. In his essay, "On 'Nation and Language,'" Bialik's discussion on translation includes a reference to an image that appears in *Don Quixote*. There, Miguel de Cervantes writes that "el traducir de una lengua en otra . . . es como quien mira los tapices flamencos por el revés" (translating from one language to another . . . is like viewing the reverse side of Flemish tapestries). Bialik takes the metaphor at face value, as a "problem" of translation, but it is precisely on the reverse side of the translation tapestry that the mycelial network of a text is made visible. And though my own scholarly work on translation acknowledges that fact, I observed in my early drafts an inclination to smooth over the rough edges of Nguyen's grammar. I added commas and periods, rearranged the syntax of a poem to make its lines more "accessible." And then, like unraveling a sweater thread, I undid this work and started over again.

In the editing stage, I spent a lot of time thinking about punctuation, and how punctuation directs and misdirects our reading of a poem. I thought about how it colludes with the expectation that translations be "fluid" and "elegant." The translatability of punctuation is often taken for granted—the idea that a period in the original can appear in the same place in the translation—but the reality is that punctuation conventions vary a great deal between languages. A comma in Hebrew does not necessarily do the same kind of work or carry the same effect as a comma in English. In fact, Hebrew has its own varied ways of indicating points of connection and disruption that don't always require the use of punctuation. This fact alone necessitated finding other solutions in English, and sometimes this translated into more or fewer commas and periods, and in others, the addition of dashes. There is no capitalization in Hebrew, but because Nguyen employs periods, I initially fell into the habit of capitalizing the first word that followed a period. Doing so, I realized, gave the impression that periods mark the beginning and end of a "sentence," which is not always the case in poetry, where this punctuation mark can signify an assertive break or pause independent of its more conventional function. In the book before you, you will see that I sometimes switch between capitalizing and not capitalizing the first letter of a line, the latter in order to give a line the feeling of a fragment or unfinished thought, as it does in my reading of the Hebrew.

That being the case, I did not want to do away with Nguyen's poetic "sentences" entirely, because the periods in her poems also set the expectation that the preceding lines are connected somehow, that something grammatical is taking place. But threading these lines together often results in entirely ungrammatical and disjointed sentences, and that is the point. Nguyen also challenges normative Hebrew grammar in other ways, for example, in her intentional misuse of prepositions (particularly those that are attached to certain verbs) and her tendency to eschew *et*, Hebrew's definite direct object particle (a feature that reminded me of early twentieth century

Hebrew poetry). It wasn't always possible to replicate these moments in the English, but given the outsized attention given to the "mistakes" of translators, these moments in the Hebrew gave my English the permission to stumble and stray.

My translation of *The Truffle Eye* includes all of the poems from *Eyn ha-kemihin* more or less following the order in which they appear in the book. I wanted to resist what I see as a proclivity in literary translation to curate book-length collections into a poet's "greatest hits." I wanted readers to experience *all* of the poems of *The Truffle Eye*—and more. Readers familiar with the Hebrew version will notice that "Winter City Poem" and the short untitled poem that follows are additions to the book. Both poems were published online but did not appear in the chapbook or book. I liked the idea of closing the poetry section with a poem that brought us back to Vietnam, or at least a memory of it. In this way, my translation introduces its own forking path, continuing the endless branching of the "truffle eye" network.

—Adriana X. Jacobs

The Truffle Eye
עין הכמהין

נהר הַמֶּקוֹנג

הַלַּיְלָה חָלַפְתִּי עַל שָׁלוֹשׁ מִטּוֹת
כְּמוֹ שָׁטְתִּי בַּמֶּקוֹנג
וְלָחַשְׁתִּי אֶת יְפִי הַפְּרָת וְהַחִדֶּקֶל.
מִתַּחַת לְרֶגַע הַתָּמִיד
מְחַפֶּשֶׂת
מִתַּחַת לַצִּיץ הַשְּׂמָאלִי
יֵשׁ לִי חוֹר
וְאַתָּה מְמַלֵּא אוֹתוֹ
בִּגְבָרִים אֲחֵרִים.
רֵיחַ שֶׁל בִּירָה "טַייגֶר"
עַל גּוּפְךָ.

בַּבְּדִידוּת,
יֵשׁ רַעַשׁ צְרָצָרִים מִדָּרוֹם לְלָאוֹס.
מַמְטֵרוֹת שֶׁל אֲוִיר קַר מֵהַאֲנוֹי
הַגַּב מִתְנַשֵּׁף
הַיַּשְׁבָן מְהֻדָּק; כֶּתֶם דְּיוֹ עַל הַבֶּטֶן.
צַיֵּר לִי תַּרְשִׁים זְרִימָה
בְּצֶבַע אֶחָד
עַל פְּרָחִים טְרִיִּים
בָּאֲגַרְטָל.

Mekong River

Tonight I moved between three beds
like I was sailing on the Mekong
and whispered the beauty of the Tigris and the Euphrates.
Under an endless moment
looking
below the left tit
I have a hole
and you fill it
with other men.
Notes of Tiger beer
on your body.

Alone,
crickets drone south of Laos.
Showers of cold air from Hanoi
the back gasps
the tight ass, an ink stain on the belly.
Sketch me a monochrome
flow chart
on fresh
potted flowers.

אֲשַׁפֵּךְ לְמַרְגְּלוֹתֶיךָ שָׁרָשִׁים,
רוֹצָה לִגְמֹר לְהָקִיא גַּרְגְּרֵי
אָבָק
בְּעֶרְוָתִי. הַנַּח אֶת יָדְךָ
בְּתוֹךְ תַּחְתּוֹנַי. תִּהְיֶה אִישִׁי
מִי מֵעֵז לַעֲזֹב מַחֲלָה בְּאֶמְצַע יָם?

I'll release roots at your feet,
I want to come to puke
specks of dust
in my crotch. Rest your hand
in my pants. Make it personal
Who dares abandon a disease mid-sea?

כאוס

מַעְיָן יוֹצֵא מֵעִיר, לְהַשְׁקוֹת אֶת הַכְּפָר
בַּדֶּרֶךְ—פֶּגֶר עַל הַכְּבִישׁ, רַמְזוֹר וּמְכוֹנִית.
מֵעַל—תְּנוּעַת מַסּוֹקִים מְאֻחָר בַּלַּיְלָה
שָׁבִים מֵהַצָּפוֹן.
אַחַר כָּךְ,
תָּבוֹא הַדֶּמוֹנִית
אַחַר כָּךְ,
בִּנְיְנֵי בֵּירוּת יִתְמוֹטְטוּ.
הַגִּיל הַזֶּה הוּא הֶמְשֵׁךְ שֶׁל מַחֲלָה, שְׁחִיטַת הַשִּׁירָה.
בּוּעָה
שֶׁל פַּרְפָּרִים גּוֹסְסִים.

Chaos

Maayan flows out of the city to water the village
On the way—roadkill, a stoplight, a car.
Overhead—helicopters hovering late at night
Coming back from the north.
Later,
          the girl from Dimona arrives.
Later,
          buildings in Beirut collapse.
This age is an ongoing epidemic, poetry's slaughter.
A bubble
of dying butterflies.

עיבוד נתונים

אַתָּה קוֹרֵא שִׁירָה
מִתְחַכֶּמֶת
מֵהֶרְצְלִיָּה פִּתּוּחַ, קָרוֹב לַיָּם.
הָיִיתָ טַיָּס עִם שֶׁבַע גִּיחוֹת לְשֶׁטַח אוֹיֵב, פַּעַם.
חַיַּי:
תְּקוּפוֹת גְּבָרִים. טַבּוּלָה רָסָה
שֶׁל רְשִׁימוֹת זַיִן.

Data Processing

You read the smart poetry
Coming out of Herzliya Pituach, near the beach.
Once, you were a pilot with seven strikes on enemy territory.
My life:
Seasons of men. A dick list
Wiped clean.

תל מילים

הָעִיר הַזּוֹ
חָבִית סְחוּבָה שֶׁל רֶפֶשׁ נִזְלָג
תֵּל מִלִּים
וְכָעֵת הַיֵּאוּשׁ

אַתָּה מֵרִיחַ אֶצְלִי אֶת הַסִּיגַרְיוֹת
אֶת הַבִּירָה בֶּטַח תִּזְהֶה
עַל פִּי הַקֶּצֶף הַלָּבָן
שֶׁעַל סְנָטֵרִי
בּוֹהֶה בָּהָר הָאָדֹם
הַרְבֵּה זְמַן הוּא לֹא הִתְפּוֹגֵג.
רָצִיתִי מִמְּךָ יוֹתֵר, אַתָּה יוֹדֵעַ
שֶׁרָצִיתִי מִמְּךָ כָּל כָּךְ יוֹתֵר.

בְּיוֹם שִׁשִּׁי
נִשְׁכַּב עַל הַחוֹף וְאֶשְׁאַב אוֹתְךָ עִם צִנּוֹר

Tell

That city—
a dank barrel of sludge
a tell of words
and now despair

You smell cigarettes on me
and guess which beer
from the white foam
on my chin
fixed on this mountain of a man
who hasn't worn off yet.
I wanted more from you, you know
that I wanted from you so much more.

On Friday
we'll lie down on the beach and I'll draw you out with a pipe

באיטיות

כְּשֶׁתַּתְחִיל לְדַקְרֵר בִּי,
אֶשְׁתַּגֵּעַ

אֲנִי מִסְתַּמֶּכֶת עַל הָאִישׁ שֶׁמּוּלִי.
כָּעֵת הוּא עָצוּב
עַל הַצָּרְפָתִיָּה הַהִיא
וְהָרוּחַ הַקְּרִירָה וְהַיַּיִן אָדֹם
הַכֹּל בְּכִכָּר מָסָרִיק מַרְגִּישׁ עָצוּב
"זֶה הַסְּתָו", נִסִּיתִי לְהַסְבִּיר.

הָעֶרֶב יָכֹלְתִּי לִרְאוֹת תַּעְתּוּעִים לָקוֹנִיִּים.
קִבַּלְתִּי זֵר עָלִים.
בְּאִטִּיוּת
מִתְוַצֶּרֶת הָאוֹבְּסֶסְיָה.

הָעֲנָפִים
הִתְחַמְּשׁוּת
בְּכַף הַיָּד שֶׁלָּנוּ
חוּטֵי עוֹר.

Slowly

When you start drilling me,
I'll go mad.

I lean on the man facing me.
He's feeling sad
about the French woman
and the cool wind and the red wine—
Everything on Masaryk Square feels sad.
"It's the fall," I tried to explain.

Tonight, I could see the terse illusions.
I received a crown of leaves.
Slowly
the obsession is made.

The branches
ammunition
lining
our palms.

רוחות

תַּקְשִׁיב לָעִיר הַזּוֹ
מֵעַל הָאֲמָרוֹת, תִּכְתֹּב מַה הַכֹּל אוֹמֵר
כְּשֶׁהֵם כּוֹתְבִים אֶת מַה
שֶׁהֵם חוֹשְׁבִים
שֶׁהֵם רוֹצִים.

וְהַשִּׁירִים, הַאִם זֶה חֵלֶק מֵהַקּוֹל?

עַל הָעוֹר הַזֶּה הִתְמַתְּחוּ אֲחֵרִים
רְעָשִׁים מְאָבְנִים מֵהַבֹּקֶר שֶׁל

הַלְּאַחַר

פִּזּוּר שֵׂעָר עַל הַכַּר,
הַהִתְכּוֹפְפוּת הַמְּהָרְהֶרֶת הַזּוֹ
שֶׁמְּטֻטֶּלֶת לִפְנֵי הַמִּטָּה.

Winds

Listen to this city
above the talk, write down what it all means
when they are writing what
they are thinking
what they are wanting.

And the poems—is this part of the voice?

Others have stretched out over this skin
Hardened noises from the morning of

The one after

Scattered hair on the pillow,
this pensive bending
cast before the bed.

יפו ד'

נָשׁוּב אֶל מְסִבַּת הַכִּתָּה
שֶׁרְשָׁרָאוֹת נְיָר עַל הַקִּיר, יָדֵינוּ רְחוֹקוֹת
הַזְּקֵנָה צוֹפָה.
קְמֵעוֹת עַל הַדּוּכָן,
הָעֶבֶד עֲקוּר הַשָּׂפָה
נִכְנָס לַכֶּלֶא.

אֲנַחְנוּ כִּלְבִים עַל הַגַּב
מוּל הַשֶּׁמֶשׁ, מוּל הָרֶב,
הַסַּף מִתְמַלֵּא, כָּרִיּוֹת נוֹי
מִחוּץ לָעִיר, שָׁרָב.

שׁוּב צְרִצָרִים בָּרֹאשׁ
וּמְלַקֵּט אוֹתָם. הִדְקַתְּ צָמוֹת
שֶׁהִצְלִיבוּ אֶת עֵינִי,
וְתוֹלָעִים
מֵרָחוֹק.

שׁוּב עַל הַמִּטָּה הַזּוֹ
לֹא יִישַׁן שׁוּם אָהוּב.
זוֹכֶרֶת
שֶׁדִּקְלַמְנוּ אֶת הָאָלֶף-בֵּית
בָּאִטְלִיז
קָנִינוּ בְּשָׂרִים בְּחֶמְלָה

Jaffa D

We'll go back to the class party
paper chains along the wall, our hands are far away
the old lady stares.
Amulets on the podium,
the slave torn from language
enters the jail.

We are dogs on their backs
facing the sun, facing the rabbi
the threshold fills, throw pillows
outside of the city, a heatwave.

Again—crickets in the head
and you chopped them off. You tightened the braids
crossing my eyes,
and the worms
           far away.

On this bed
no lover will sleep again.
You remember
that we recited the alphabet
At the butcher's
we bought meat with mercy.

אִידֵיאָל

עוֹד מְעַט הִיא תִּנְטֹף, עוֹד מְעַט
תִּזָּרֵק כֵּס לִצְעֹק
"זֶה טֵרוּף!"
זוֹ פְּסִיכִית זוֹ
תּוֹעֲבַת מְכַשֵּׁפוֹת
עֲטַלֵּף מְמַהֵר לַחֲצוֹת רָקִיעַ
מִתַּחַת אוֹיֵב בּוּרְגָּנִי עַל מִזְרָן.

מֵאָה אָחוּז תְּשׂוּמֶת-לֵב
כְּמוֹ אוֹהֵב, אִידֵיאָל
שׁוֹשְׁבִין הַנְּסִיכוּת הַיִּשְׂרְאֵלִית.
מִתַּחַת לְמִסְגֶּרֶת הָעֵץ
שֶׁל הַתְּמוּנָה הָרְקוּמָה
בְּלִי הַקִּירוֹת שֶׁמִּסָּבִיב, אַתָּה עַכְשָׁו
רַק תִּמְהוֹנִי
מְשׁוֹטֵט
עִם כּוֹבַע.

Ideal

Soon she'll drip, soon
she'll throw a chair screaming
"This is crazy!"
This mental case
A witches' scourge
A bat cutting across the sky
Underneath, a bourgeois enemy on a mattress.

One-hundred percent present
like a lover, the ideal
best man of Israeli princes.
Under the wooden frame
of an embroidered picture
with no walls around, you're now
just an eccentric
prowling around
with a hat.

אתה יודע מה יהיה?

שְׁקִיפוּת הַבֹּקֶר
בִּשְׁלִיפַת-תֵּיוֹן
תּוֹסֵס,
גַּרְגִּירֵי צִ'ילִי עַל הָאוֹמְלֶט.
כְּשֶׁאֶתְכּוֹפֵף לְפָנֶיךָ
כְּנָפַיִם מְטוֹת לְאָחוֹר

אֲוַירֵר לְמַעַנְךָ,
חַיָּל, בַּעַל כָּמְתָּה, דַּרְגָּה וְשׁוֹט
עַד שֶׁעֵינַי יִרְתְּחוּ
מוּל תַּרְבּוּת הַדָּרוֹם,
חֶבֶל
שֶׁל אֶרֶץ גַּסָּה.

Do You Know What's Coming?

Morning transparency
drawing out
a sparkling teabag,
an omelet with chili flakes.
When I bend before you
a pair of wings stretch back

I'll drool just for you,
soldier, master of beret, rank, and whip,
until my eyes boil
before this southern culture,
the rope
of a rough country.

מעין

הֵם נִפְגָּשִׁים בְּלֵב הָעִיר, בּוֹהֵמָה עִבְרִית,
לְתַכְנֵן מַעְיָן שׁוֹפֵעַ בַּסֶּנְטְרַל שֶׁל הַפְּאַרְק.
אֵיפֹה הַשֶּׁלֶג שֶׁל אֶתְמוֹלהָאֶשְׁתָּקַד?
שָׁאַל וִילוֹן
בַּתְּקוּפָה שֶׁהַמִּלִּים
הִתְעַלּוּ מֵעַל הֲנָאוֹת הַגּוּף,
לִפְנֵי שֶׁצָּמְחוּ כָּל גּוֹרְדֵי הַשְּׁחָקִים.

Maayan

They meet at the heart of this Hebrew bohème
to compose a flowing fountain in the central park
But where are the snows of yester-year?
asked Villon
back then when words
transcended the body's pleasures,
before all the skyscrapers grew.

לולאה

לַחְכּוֹת לִמְאַהֵב בֵּינַיִם מַסְנִיף שַׁרְשֶׁרֶת מוּזִיקָלִית,
שֶׁעַמּוּם זֶה
אִינֶרְצְיָה שֶׁל רַגְלַיִם מִתְאַהֲבוֹת
שֶׁנִּתְעַטְּפוּ וְהִתְלַפְּפוּ
בְּהִזְדַּקְּרוּת שֶׁל מַסְפִּיק
מִדַּי
גְּבָרִים
הָעֶרֶב.
בְּמִאוּס, בְּתִעוּב שֶׁל בָּלוֹן.
אֲנִי קָטָלוֹג בְּגָדִים
אִישִׁיּוּת דּוּ-קְטָבִית
בָּעִיר הַזּוֹ אֲנִי
דֻּכָּאוֹן מְהֻדָּקֶת עַל עֵץ.

Loop

Waiting for the rebound lover sniffing a medley
This boredom is
The inertia of legs in love
Enveloped and coiled
At a standstill of no
More
Men
Tonight.
Repulsed, with a balloon's loathing
I am a fashion catalog
A bipolar personality
In this city I am
A depression clamped against a tree.

כתם תרבות

תַּחְקֹר לִפְנֵי שֶׁתִּקְטֹף
זְרָעִים שֶׁל הֶבֶל אֵצֶל הַגָּדָה
בְּרוּחַ הַכְּפָר
וְהַדְּרָכִים
וְהָלְאָה.

בָּאֹפֶק הַכְּנִיסָה לָעִיר, נַיָּד נִשָּׂא
מְשׁוֹרֵר שַׁעֲוָה בְּלִי פַּטְרוֹן
בְּלִי פֶּנְזִין.

שֶׁמֶשׁ וְרֻדָּה שׁוֹקַעַת
בְּעֵינֶיךָ אֲגַם מוּזִיקָלִי שֶׁל מוֹנֶהְבַּאךְ
כְּשֶׁנִּתְחַבֵּק
תִּשְׁאַל מֵאֵיפֹה בָּאתִי. אָשִׁיב,
בָּאתִי מֵהָרַכֶּבֶת.
מֵאֵיפֹה בָּאתִי, אַתָּה שׁוֹאֵל
כְּלוֹמַר, הַהוֹרִים?

Culture Stain

Examine before you extract
the seeds of nothing at the riverbank
with the village air
and the roads
and so on.

In the horizon, the city begins, a portable
wax poet without a patron
or fanzine.

A rosy sun sets
on a musical Monetbach lake in your eyes—
When we hold each other
you'll ask where I came from. I'll say
I came from this rot.
Where did I come from, you're asking,
I mean, parents?

פרקי מטרופולין

עֲזֹב אֶת הַבִּנְיָנִים הַגְּבוֹהִים מֵעָלֵינוּ
אוֹתָנוּ שֶׁיּוֹשְׁבִים עַל מִכְסֶה בִּיּוּב, מֵאֲחוֹרֵי הַשֵּׁרוּתִים שֶׁל הָרְחוֹב.
עֲזֹב אֶת כָּל הַתְּרוּפוֹת
וְהַמַּעֲטֶפֶת הַלְּבָנָה
שֶׁנּוֹעֶלֶת אוֹתְךָ
בְּצַד הַמִּדְרָכָאִים.
סְלִילִים שֶׁל סֶלוֹטֵייפּ לָבָן.

אַתָּה, תִּשְׂכֹּר לִי דִּירָה
עִם חֲדַר כְּתִיבָה בָּעִיר
אַכְרִיחַ אוֹתְךָ לִכְתֹּב כָּל יוֹם שִׁיר עָלַי
אַתָּה תִּכְתֹּב שִׁיר עָלַי
כְּמוֹ שֶׁאָמַרְתָּ שֶׁאַתָּה אוֹהֵב אֶצְלִי אֶת הַיֵּאוּשׁ
אָמַרְתָּ שֶׁזֶּה מַקְסִים.

Metropolitan Pieces

Leave the buildings towering over us,
squatting on a manhole cover, behind the public toilets.
Leave the meds
and the white coat
that locks you in
with these depressives.
Spools of white scotch tape.

You—find me a place in the city
with a room to write
I'll make you write a poem about me every day
You will write a poem about me
Like you said what you love about me is the desperation
It's brilliant you said.

שיר ללא שם

הַבֹּקֶר מִבַּעַד לִשְׁאֵרִית הַוִּילוֹן
שֶׁאָכַל הֶעָשׁ
שֶׁתָּלָה אָדָם
שֶׁנָּגַר לְבַד עִם
אֲדָנִיּוֹת קְבָרִים בַּמִּרְפֶּסֶת.

אֲנִי מְאֹהֶבֶת בִּרְשִׁימַת הַסְּפָרִים שֶׁלְּךָ.
מְאֹהֶבֶת בְּךָ;
רֵיחַ הָעִזָּבוֹן
כְּבָר בַּחֹשֶׁךְ.

Untitled

This morning through the remains of a curtain
that a moth ate
that a man draped
living alone with
grave planters on the balcony.

I'm in love with your book catalogue.
And in love with you—
the scent of a bequest
gone dark.

הרצליה

אֶתְמוֹל, בִּזְמַן שֶׁשִּׂחַקְנוּ
רָצִיתִי שֶׁתִּקַּח סַכִּין
וּבִצְחוֹק
כְּאִלּוּ אֲמִתִּי
אֲבָל בֶּאֱמֶת;

הֶרְצֵלִיָּה הִיא
הָרְעָשִׁים מִחוּץ לַחַלּוֹן.
מַדָּפִים רוֹקַנְתִּי
לְהַחֲזִיר לַמָּקוֹם, לִסְגֹּר אֶת הַדֶּלֶת
לִפְנֵי הַשֵּׁנָה.

עוֹד לֹא אָמַרְתָּ לִי "אַל תִּהְיִי עֲצוּבָה כְּשֶׁנִּסְתַּיֵּם"
וְעוֹד לֹא אָמַרְתָּ, כַּמָּה טוֹב זֶה הָיָה.
הַמִּשְׁפָּחָה וְהַחֲבֵרוֹת—בְּמֶרְחַק עִיר, בְּסַךְ הַכֹּל.
בְּמֶרְחָק שֶׁל עִיר! לְמַעֲשֶׂה.

"אַל תַּגִּידִי אֶת זֶה", (אָמַרְתָּ שֶׁזֶּה מַחֲלִישׁ אוֹתִי)
הִתְרַגַּלְתִּי
לִחְיוֹת
אֶצְלְךָ
בְּתוֹךְ
הַבֶּטֶן;
אֲדָנִית קְטַנָּה שֶׁל צֶמַח תַּאֲוָה.

Herzliya

Yesterday, while we were playing
I wanted you to grab a knife
and playfully
like it was real
but really—

Herzliya is
the noise outside a window.
I emptied the shelves
to put back in place, to close the door
before going to bed.

You still didn't say "Don't be sad when we're done"
and you still didn't say how good it was.
Family and girlfriends—in the end, they are a city away.
A whole city away! Actually.

"Don't say that" (you said it weakens me)
I got used to
living
with you
in
the belly—
a little planter of aphrodisiacs.

זוכרת זכרותך

זוֹכֶרֶת שֶׁרָצִיתָ
מִשְׁפָּט שֶׁל אָנֶס עַל דַּרְגַּשׁ עֵץ.
לִשְׁבֹּר אֶת הַקֶּרַח
עַכְשָׁו נִתְנַשֵּׁק
אֲנִי זוֹכֶרֶת זַכְרוּתְךָ בַּזִּכְרוֹנוֹת.

אֵיךְ תִּהְיֶה רוֹמַנְטִיקָה —
כְּשֶׁנִּשְׁכַּב מְאֻזָּנִים
מְרֻתָּקִים לַזְּמַן? בּוֹדְדִים מֵהַדִּיּוּנוֹת
שֶׁל אַפְרִיקָה הַגְּדוֹלָה. אֶל גּוֹרְדֵי-הַשְּׁחָקִים
נְיוּ יוֹרְק. נְיוּ יוֹרְק.
אֲהַפֹּךְ אֶת הַלֵּב
תַּהֲפֹךְ לִי אֶת הַבֶּטֶן
אַחֲרֵי זֶה נִתְאַהֵב.

Remembering Your Member

Remembering that you wanted
a rape sentence on a wooden pallet.
To break the ice
now we'll kiss
I remember your member with these memories.

How will it turn romantic—
When we lie horizontal
in the thrall of time? Loners out of the dunes
of great Africa. To the skyscrapers—
New York. New York.
I'll turn my heart
You'll turn my stomach.
After that we'll fall for each other.

מאמרים בטירול

גָּבוֹהַּ בֵּין הָעֲנָנִים בְּמִינוּס שָׁלוֹשׁ מַעֲלוֹת
זֶה מִשְׁתַּנֶּה
לְאֹרֶךְ הַכְּבִישׁ נוֹסְעִים הַחוּצָה מִמִּינְכֶן,
וְהַחַלּוֹן לָבָן וְהַשֶּׁמֶשׁ לְבָנָה.
הָעֲנָנִים קְשׁוּרִים בְּחוּט
וּמַנְמִיכִים אֶל תּוֹכָם.
אֶל
הָרָקוּם
רְפוּדִים.
סֻכָּרִיּוֹת זְכוּכִית מְתוּקוֹת
רוֹעֲשׁוֹת עַל הַלְּשׁוֹנוֹת,

חֹרֶף בְּטִירוֹל
וְאִשָּׁה מִסְתּוֹבֶבֶת עֵירֻמָּה בְּ"גוֹלְדֶן הִירְשׁ",
גּוֹרֶסֶת מִיצֵי פֵרוֹת.
אוֹמֶרֶת:
שַׁק לִי בַּדְּגְדּוּגִים וְכַמָּה זַלְצְבּוּרְג יָפָה.

Tyrolean Essays

High between the clouds at -3 degrees
it changes
they drive along the road outside of Munich
and the window is white and the sun is white.
The clouds are threaded together
and lower into them.
Into
the embroidered
upholstery—
Sweet glass candies
clamor on their tongues.

Winter in Tyrol
and at the Goldener Hirsch a woman goes around naked
grinding fruit juice.
She says:
Kiss my clit and *Salzburg is so pretty.*

שלוש תמונות מפריז

1

עַל סַפְסָל צָרְפָתִי בַּגַּנָּה
אִמָּא צוֹעֶקֶת עַל יֶלֶד חוֹרֵג,
הוּא טוֹבֵל אֶת הַיָּד בַּמִּזְרָקָה.

מִישֶׁהוּ מְעַשֵּׁן ג'וֹינְט.
מַקִּיף אֶת עֵינָיו, לְהַסְתִּירָן
מִבֵּין הָעֲנָנִים
קֶרֶן
אוֹגוּסְט קוּבִּיסְטִית.

2

אוֹגוּסְט עַל
טַיֶּלֶת הַשַּׁאנְז אֱלִיזֶה
דּוֹפֵק בְּרֶחֶם.
הֵקֵאתִי סִיגַרְיּוֹת עַל קַבְצָן יָשֵׁן
מִתַּחַת
יָרֵחַ עָגֹל
עַל מִסְגֶּרֶת קַרְטוֹן.
שׁוּב
אַתָּה
נִצְמָד אֵלַי מוּל טִפּוֹת וְרַעַשׁ
יְלָלָה מוּל בָּתִּים גֶּרְמָנִיִּים.

Three Snapshots of Paris

1

On a French park bench
a mother screams as the step-child
dips his hand into the fountain.

Someone's smoking a joint.
He shields his eyes—
Between the clouds
a cubist
August beam.

2

August on
the promenade of the Champs-Élysées
knocks on the womb.
I threw up cigarettes on a beggar sleeping
under
a full moon
on a cardboard frame.
Again
you
cling to me with the drizzle and loud
howling in front of German houses.

יֵשׁ צְלָלִיּוֹת עַל סַפְסָלִים
וְאַתָּה נוֹטֵף דְּמָעוֹת אֲרָיוֹת,
נוֹשֵׁךְ אוֹתִי בְּקִנְאַת-סוֹפֵר
נוֹשֵׁךְ בַּגַּב, חָזָק.
עִם הַשִּׁנַּיִם פּוֹרֵס
וְהָעֶלְבּוֹן, מְחוּץ לַמִּרְפָּסוֹת הַבּוֹהֲמִיּוֹת.
הִנֵּה הַגּוּף שֶׁלָּנוּ
מַרְצָפוֹת מִדְרָכוֹת שֶׁל כְּבִישִׁים.
הִנֵּה עֵינַי בְּעָרְפִּי
תִּרְאֶה, יַקִּירִי, אֵיךְ אֲנַחְנוּ
עַתִּיקִים כְּמוֹ פָּרִיז,
אֵיךְ עוֹד
תַּחֲלם עָלַי שׁוּב
בְּעֶצֶב.

3
גֶּשֶׁם אָפוּי בְּסִירוֹפ גְּרֶנְד מֶרְנְיֶיה
מְרִיחִים בָּצָל וְלַשְׁלֶשֶׁת יוֹנִים.
אֵיפֹה עֲלִיַּת הַגַּג
אֵיפֹה הַתִּקְרָה הַמְחֻדֶּדֶת
בַּשָּׁעָה שֶׁל פָּרִיז, עַל גְּדוֹת הַסֵּיין.

40

Shadows rest on these benches
and you weep lion tears
and bite me with literary envy,
bite down hard on my back.
With pique and teeth
chomping on the bohemian balconies.
Behold, our body is
this tiled street pavement.
Behold, I have eyes on my back.
Look, darling, we are
as old as Paris
and still
you'll dream about me
with regret.

3
Rain baked with Grand Marnier
gives off notes of onion and pigeon shit.
Where is the attic—
Where is the vaulted ceiling—
in Paris time, on the banks of the Seine.

הוליווד

שׁוּם דָּבָר לֹא מַגִּיעַ
אֶל תּוֹךְ חֲדַר מִלְחָמָה
טָעוּן
כּוֹכָבִים

עֲצֵי מִנִיפָה
מְטִילִים פֵּרוֹת
מֵעַל מְכוֹנִיּוֹת נוֹסְעוֹת לְרֹחַב הַטַּיֶּלֶת,
מְקָרְזָלִים עֲדַיִן עוֹמְדִים עַל רֶגֶל אַחַת
מְנַגְּנִים פְּסִיכוֹדֶלְיָה
מִתּוֹךְ אֹהֶל.

רְאֵה אוֹתִי, אֲנִי שִׁגְרָה.
בְּבֵית קָפֶה, עַל מֶלְרוֹז, בּוֹהָה בַּכְּלָבִים הַנִּמְלָטִים מִבַּעֲלֵיהֶם
עַד שֶׁהַשֶּׁמֶשׁ שָׁבָה
לְהָאִיר עַל הוֹלִיווד מַעֲרָב.

בְּמוֹרַד פָּסָדִינָה הַיְשָׁנָה,
אֲנָשִׁים מְשׁוֹטְטִים עִם מַצְלֵמָה
מוֹצָרְט בָּרַדְיוֹ, הֵם מְדַבְּרִים עַל עֲרָפֶל יוֹרֵד
מֵעַל הוֹלִיווד,
מַסְתִּיר אֶת הַשֶּׁלֶט.

Hollywood

Nothing gets into
a war room
loaded
with stars.

Palm trees
dropping fruit
on the cars along the boardwalk,
frizzy-haired yogis still standing on one leg,
playing psychedelic songs
inside a tent.

Look at me, I'm a routine.
In a café on Melrose, I'm staring at dogs running from their owners
until the sun comes back
to brighten West Hollywood.

In downtown Old Pasadena,
people wander about with a camera,
Mozart on the radio, they talk about the fog falling
over Hollywood,
hiding the sign.

אורכידאה

אַנִּיחַ גֻּלְגֹּלֶת וְאוֹרְכִידֵאָה
בֵּין הָרַגְלַיִם.
אֲנִי רוֹצָה לִמְשֹׁךְ לְךָ,
לִקְרֹעַ אֶת הַחֵךְ.

הִדְחַקְנוּ אֶת עַצְמֵנוּ
אֶל הַגְּרוּטָאָה הָאֲדָמָה
עַל שְׂפָתַי
מַעֲטֶפֶת קוֹרְדֶּרוֹי מְטֻנֶּפֶת, אַשְׁפַּת הָרְחוֹב
וּנְהָמָה עָלְתָה בָּהּ
קָרְאָה: אֲנִי פְלוֹרֶנְטִין!

Orchid

I'll rest a skull and orchid
between my legs.
I want to draw you in
and rend the palate.

We repressed
to the red wreck
on my lips
a filthy corduroy clutch, street trash
a roar rose in there
and cried out: *I am Florentin!*

מנהטן

קָרָה בַּחֲצוֹת מֵעַל הַגַּגּוֹת; טְנֹפֶת
מִתְרוֹצֶצֶת בָּרְחוֹבוֹת לְצַד מוֹנִיּוֹת.
אִישׁ חוֹצֶה אֶת הַכְּבִישׁ.
עוֹד שֶׁלֶד גּוֹרֵד שְׁחָקִים
נֶעֱטָף בְּנַיְלוֹן וְרֶשֶׁת בִּטָּחוֹן.
פָּנָס מֵאִיר
עַל בֶּטוֹן בִּנְסִיקָה.

רָצִיתִי לְכַסּוֹת אוֹתְךָ וְרָכַבְתִּי אֶל הָאַכָּף,
לְאַזֵּן אֶת הַשִּׁיאִים.
חָשַׁבְתִּי שֶׁאֲנִי מוּכָנָה לְקַצֵּץ בַּפְּלוּמָה שֶׁמִּתַּחַת לַגַּרְגֶּרֶת,
בְּצַמְתֵּי הַשְּׂדֵרוֹת חוֹלְפִים עַל פְּנֵי הָמוֹן רַב.
יֵשׁ אַשְׁפַּת תַּעֲשִׂיָּה בָּרְחוֹבוֹת הָרְחָבִּיִּים.
עִם הַמִּגְדָּלִים הַמִּתְנַשְּׂאִים
אֲפִלּוּ הַכְּנֵסִיּוֹת בְּלוֹנְדִינִיּוֹת.

אוּלַי זֶה יַעֲזֹר אִם נְדַמְיֵן: אֵיךְ הָרֹאשׁ מְפַזֵּר
אֶת פְּסוֹת הַפֶּסֶל
עַל הַלֵּב
לִרְקֹחַ
רַבַּת שַׁעַטְנֵז!

Manhattan

It happened at midnight on the rooftops—filth
runs down the streets next to the taxis.
A man crosses the road.
Another skeleton skyscraper
wrapped in nylon and a security network.
A lamp glows
over rising concrete.

I wanted to cover you up and rode to the saddle point,
to balance the peaks.
I thought I was ready to clip the fuzz under the Adam's apple,
at intersections one passes over the masses.
There's industrial waste in the transverse streets.
Next to these rising towers
even the churches are blonde.

Maybe it would help to picture this: how the head scatters
sculptural scraps
over the heart
to cook up
a hybrid jam!

הֵיכָן שֶׁיָּשַׁנּוּ עַל סַפְסָל

זָנָב לַהֲמוֹנִים בֵּין כָּל כָּךְ
אֱלֹהִים.
עַל מִשְׁטַח הָעֵץ נַיְלוֹן רָטֹב
שְׁלוּלִיּוֹת מְתוּחוֹת בְּלוֹנְג אַיְלֶנְד.
מִסָּבִיב, נְסִיכוֹת בְּשֶׁקֶט נוֹירוֹטִי.

אֲנִי
סְפוֹג קָטָן
מָלֵא סְכוֹת
בִּטָּחוֹן.

בְּבֵית הַכְּנֶסֶת, פִּנַּת הַקָּדוֹשׁ. לְיַד הַמָּשִׁיחַ, לְיַד בְּרוֹדְוֵוי!
הֵיכָן שֶׁשָּׂרַפְתִּי אֶת הַתִּקְרָה. הֵיכָן שֶׁיָּשַׁנּוּ עַל סַפְסָל
כִּסִּינוּ אֶת פָּנֵינוּ בַּחֲלָצוֹת. הִגַּשְׁתִּי לְחִי שְׁנִיָּה
מַשַּׁט שְׂמִיכַת מַתֶּכֶת
מֵעַל הַהַדְסוֹן.

Where We Slept on a Bench

A tail for the crowds between so much
God.
Wet nylon on a wooden surface
tense puddles in Long Island.
All around, a neurotic silence of princesses.

I am
a tiny sponge
full of safety
pins.

At the synagogue, the holy corner. Next to the Messiah, next
to Broadway!
Where I set fire to the ceiling. Where we slept on a bench
and covered our faces with shirts. I turned my other cheek
a flotilla of sheet metal
on the Hudson.

מעל ההדסון

וְהָיָה אִישׁ רָץ אֶל הָרַכֶּבֶת וְהָרַכֶּבֶת נוֹסַעַת.
כָּעֵת,
הָאִישׁ זוֹעֵף.
אִם לֹא הָיָה רָץ אֶל הָרַכֶּבֶת—רוּחוֹ הָיְתָה טוֹבָה.
וְהָיִיתִי אֲנִי, שֶׁנָּסַגְתִּי אֶל הָעַצְלוּת
רָחַצְתִּי אֶת הַצִּפָּרְנַיִם
הֵסַרְתִּי אֶת הַלִּכְלוּךְ.

אַתָּה עֲדַיִן
גּוֹרֵם לִי לִרְצוֹת
לְהַחְדִּיר גַּרְזֶן לַמֹּחַ.

עַל הַגַּג,
לְצַד הָאַנְטֶנָה וְגַדְלוּת הַמַּבָּט—
אֶכְתֹּב אֶת הָרוֹמָן שֶׁלִּי;

אֵיךְ הָיוּ סִירֶנוֹת בָּרֶקַע
בְּרָקִים מֵעַל הַהַדְסוֹן.

On the Hudson

A man ran after the train but the train keeps going.
And now
       he's furious.
Had he not run after the train—he was in a good mood.
But I was the one withdrawing into apathy
scrubbing my nails
and shedding the dirt.

You still
make me want
to drive an axe into my head.

On the rooftop,
by the antenna and a bigger view—
I will write my novel:

How there were sirens in the background
and lightning on the Hudson.

ילד יהודי

בּוֹא נִסַּע עַד הֲלוֹם
נִסַּע דֶּרֶךְ הַמּוֹשָׁבוֹת
צֹמֶת גְּדֵרָה פְּקוּקָה.

הַפָּזָה הַזּוֹ הִיא אֵירוֹפֵּאִית
אֲבָל הִיא בּוֹלְשֶׁבִיקִית
מִשּׁוּם
הַוֶּסְט הַצַּמְרִירִי וְרַעֲמַת הַתַּלְתַּלִּים
הַזְּהֻבָּה. תְּכֵלוֹת הֵן עֵינֶיךָ, יֶלֶד יְהוּדִי בְּמוֹסְקְבָה
מִתְחַזֶּה לְצָאר
שׁוֹתֶה וֹדְקָה מִכּוֹסִית קְרִיסְטָל
מְרַחְרֵחַ בֵּיצֵי סַלְמוֹן עַל קְרֶקֶר, וְהַשֵּׁם מִדְגָּשׁ זָהָב
בְּתוֹךְ הַקָּנוֹן.

בַּדִּירָה, רֵיחַ שֶׁל דַּפִּים מְחֻנוּת יָד שְׁנִיָּה.
אַתָּה מַנִּיחַ אֶת הָרֶגֶל בְּהִסּוּס
וְאָז טוֹבֵל אֶת כָּל גּוּפְךָ בָּאַמְבַּטְיָה
"תַּדְלִיקִי לִי סִיגַרְיָה, הִנֵּה הַחֲפִיסָה עַל הָרִצְפָּה"
מַצְבִּיעַ וְנוֹטֵף,

וּבְפָנֶיךָ הַזּוֹלְגוֹת גֶּבֶר.

52

Jewish Boy

Let's drive to Ad Halom
through the villages
Gedera junction is jammed.

This is the European phase
but Bolshevik
with the fleece vest
and the mane of golden curls.
You blue-eyed, Jewish boy from Moscow
making like a czar
drinking vodka from a crystal glass
sniffing salmon roe on a cracker, and your gilded name
in the holy canon.

The apartment smells like paper from a second-hand store.
You lower a tentative leg
and then dip your whole body into the bathtub
"Give me a light, the pack is on the floor"
you point and drip

and in your face, a man flows.

בְּכְבִישׁ מִסְפָּר אַחַת, אָמֶרִיקָה נִצֶּבֶת עַל קַת
פְּסְגַּת הָהָר מוֹרִיקָה
יָד וָשֵׁם.

אוֹסֶפֶת תּוֹלָעִים
לִתְפֹּר עֲבוּרֵךְ שׁוֹשֶׁלֶת
וּמָסֹרֶת.
הֵיכָן שֶׁאֲנִי מְשׁוֹטֶטֶת
בָּרְחוֹבוֹת
מְחַכָּה לָאַבְּסוּרְד.
בַּדֶּרֶךְ אֶצְמַח
בַּדֶּרֶךְ אֶקְמֹל.
זֵר זְרָדִים מֵעַל הָרֹאשׁ.

Highway 1

On Highway 1, America's fixed on a gun—
The hilltop greening
a place and a name.

Gathering worms
to stitch an ancestry for you
and a tradition.
On the streets
where I wander
I am waiting for the absurd.
On the way I'll grow—
On the way I'll wither—
Twigs crowning my head.

נוף אחרון

צְבִיטָה שֶׁל נוֹף
עַל כְּבִישׁ לָה גְּוַוארְדְיָה.

אַתָּה שׁוֹלֵחַ זְרוֹעַ שְׁלֵמָה
אֶל תּוֹךְ הַצַּלֶּקֶת שֶׁבֵּין הָעַמּוּדִים, בְּטָוַח הַבִּנְיָנִים
מִתַּחַת לַגֶּשֶׁר.
וְכָכָה יָדְךָ מִסְתַּדֶּרֶת
כָּכָה אַתָּה נִשְׁעָן עַל שְׂפָתַי.

The Last Landscape

A pinch of landscape
on LaGuardia St.

You elbow deep
into the scar between the pages, in building range
under the bridge.
And that's how your hand gets by
that's how you lean on my lips.

שיר הנווד

אֵינוֹ רוֹכֵב עַל חַיָּה עִם פְּרָסוֹת.
הוּא מַעֲדִיף לְהַטְרִיד אֶת רֹאשׁוֹ
לַעֲמֹד מְרֻפָּט לְצַד דֶּרֶךְ
תַּחַת עֵץ
לְחַכּוֹת
אֵיךְ יִשְׂרֹד אַחֲרֵי כְּמוֹ צְטוּט.
הַיּוֹם נֵלֵךְ אֶל עָרִים אֲחֵרוֹת

בִּגְבוּל הַמְּדִינָה, שָׂדוֹת וּבָתִּים.
בַּכְּנִיסָה לְכָל עִיר
כְּתֹבֶת רְשׁוּמָה עַל יְדֵי מְנַצְּחִים.
אִשָּׁה בְּסִנָּר
תֵּצֵא אֵלֵינוּ עִם חֶרֶב
תַּבִּיט בָּנוּ. קַרְחוֹנִים
וּפַעֲמוֹנִים יְצַלְצְלוּ.
וַעֲדַיִן הַתְּשִׁישׁוּת.
"שָׁם," הִיא תַּצְבִּיעַ לִקְרַאת הָעֶרֶב, "זֶה לֹא רָחוֹק."

Nomad Poem

He won't ride a shod animal.
He prefers to trouble his head
to stand by the road unkempt
under a tree
waiting
how he will outlive me like a quotation.
   Today we'll go to other cities

on the border of the state, fields and houses.
At the entrance of every city
there's an address written by the victors.
A woman in an apron
    will come out with a sword
and look at us. Glaciers
and bells will ring.
And still, the exhaustion.
"There," she will point as evening nears, "It's not far."

פונדק

בְּפֻנְדָּק עִם מוּסִיקָה דֶּנִית
אָמְרָה מֶלְצָרִית:
(שֶׁנִּרְאֵית כְּמוֹ כּוֹכֶבֶת פִילְם-נוּאָר) אִם
הָיָה לָהּ קַנְבַס
הָיְתָה צוֹבַעַת בְּכָתֹם
וּמְצַיֶּרֶת בְּאָפֹר
מַשֶׁהוּ
עַל שְׁאִיפוֹת.

הִיא הִגִּישָׁה סִיגַרְיוֹת הוֹדִיּוֹת בְּרֵיחַ קְטֹרֶת,
הַכֹּל בְּטַעַם זוֹל.
שׁוּב הַכֹּל רָחוֹק
וְהֵם שׂוֹרְפִים פַּחִים עַל הַכְּבִישׁ.

"גַּם אֲנִי
אָמוּת רוֹמַנְטִית," אָמְרָה,
"בְּשָׂחֹר לָבָן, מִחוּץ לַחֶדֶר
אֶצְעַד גְּבוֹהָה
עִם יְרֵשַׁת שֵׂיבָה
וַאֲבָנִים בַּכִּיס".

60

Inn

At the inn with the Danish music
the waitress (looking like a film noir star) said
that if she had a canvas
she would paint with orange
and draw with grey
something
about aspiration.

She handed over Indian cigarettes that smelled like incense,
everything tastes cheap
everything is far away again
and they're burning tin sheets in the street.

"I'm going to die romantically too," she said,
"in black and white, out of this room
I'll walk proud
with my grey hairs
and stones in my pocket."

זר מתמשך

נִדְמֶה שֶׁתִּתְעוֹפֵף כָּל רֶגַע
תַּמְצִית חֻלְשָׁתָהּ
בְּרֶגֶשׁ רִאשׁוֹנִי
וְהִיא הִתְפַּעֲלָה
מֵחֹסֶן הַזְּרוֹעַ
הַסּוּסֵי חַשְׁמַל.

עַל כָּל פָּנִים, אֲשֶׁר נָח
בְּעִרְבּוּבְיָהּ
אַבְנֵי רִצְפָּה לוֹהֲטוֹת
מִתַּחַת, תִּקְרַת סַגְרִיר.
הוּא פָּסַע אָנֶה וָאָנָה, לוֹחֵשׁ
שֶׁתַּתִּיר אֶת הַכַּפְתּוֹרִים, שֶׁתַּעֲזֹב אֶת הַבֵּינַיִם
דְּמָעוֹת שֶׁל קִרְבָה נֶאֱסָפוֹת בְּתַחְתִּית הָעַכּוּז
הִנֵּה הַזֵּעָה מַבְשִׁילָה.

Stranger Still

It looks like she could take off any minute
the essence of her weakness
was in the initial emotion
but she was moved
        by the arm's resilience
electric indecisions.

On every face, happiness settles
in her concoction
burning floor tiles
underneath, a roof of hard rain.
He stepped from here to there, whispering
that she mend the buttons, abandon the in-between
tears of intimacy gather below the buttocks
there sweat ripens.

אמסטרדם

הַדְּמָמָה תָּבוֹא,
כְּשֶׁבִּקְצוֹתֶיךָ הַזָּהָב.
תְּצַלֵּם אוֹתִי!

צַחֲנָה בַּמִּסְדְּרוֹן
וְאָמָּנוּת.
אַתָּה
דּוֹקֵר וּמַחֲרִיב וְעוֹקֵר וּסְתָו בְּאַמְסְטֶרְדַם.

צְרִיחִים מִתְרוֹמְמִים מֵעַל בִּצָּה
עֲנָפִים מַחְלִיקִים בָּהּ,
שְׁפִירִית מִתְאַזֶּנֶת לִקְרַאת סְעָרָה.

Amsterdam

The silence will arrive
when the gold reaches your edges.
Take my picture!

A stench in the hallway
and art.
You
stab and ruin and uproot and it's fall in Amsterdam.

Turrets loom over the swamp
branches glide through it
a dragonfly balances before a storm.

גבר

עֲדַיִן מְחַיֵּךְ
עֲדַיִן שׁוֹכֵב
כְּמוֹ בֻּדְהָה.

מֵהֶרֶס שֶׁחִרְרַרְתִּי
אֶת הַיֵּצֶר מִשְּׂמֹאל הַגּוּף
הִצַּגְתִּי לְפָנֶיךָ תְּאֵנָה אֲיֻמָּה,
קַדֵרַת צְפַרְדְּעִים.

Man

Still smiling
Still resting
    like a Buddha.

I unbridled
the urge from the left side of my body
I served you an awful fig,
a frog casserole.

משוררת מַסְמְרִים

בְּטֶרֶם תַּיְשִׁיר אֵלַי מַבָּט שֶׁל כְּבִישִׁים בֵּין עִירוֹנַיִים
וְתֻשַׁק לָאֶצְבַּע,
תֹּאמַר,
"זוֹ אֶצְבְּעוֹנִית חֲמוּדָה" —
אֲנִי מְבִינָה שֶׁהַסּוֹף שֶׁלָּנוּ הוּא דְּמָעוֹת וְצַעַר שָׁחֹר. כָּעֵת,
הִנֵּה אֲנַחְנוּ בְּכֹעַר הַוִּדּוּיִים;

שֶׁהַשִּׁירָה הַחֲדָשָׁה שֶׁלִּי מְלֵאַת כְּעָסִים
וַאֲנִי קִיא שִׁכְרוּתָה שֶׁל זוֹנַת הָרְגָשׁוֹת. שֶׁמְּשׁוֹרֶרֶת מַסְמְרִים!
וְהֶשַׁבְתִּי שֶׁשּׂוֹנֵאת לִכְתֹּב
אֶת יִסּוּרֶיהָ
כְּאִלּוּ רַק לִבָּהּ. לְלֹא מַעֲשִׂים שֶׁל תֹּכֶן,
רַק הַרְגָּשָׁה קָרָה.
וְאִם הָיִיתִי כּוֹתֶבֶת שִׁירָה אָז
הָיִיתִי כּוֹתֶבֶת פְּרוֹזָה.
שֶׁזֶּה הֶבְדֵּלֵי חֲרוּזִים
וְאֹרֶךְ נְשִׁימָה.

Poet of Nails

Before you give me that look of intercity roads
and kiss my finger,
you'll say,
"Darling Thumbelina"—
I get that our end will be tears and dark regret. For now,
we are on the ugly side of confession:

That my new poetry is full of rage
that I am the drunk vomit of an emotion slut. A poet of nails!
And I reply that I hate to write
her torments
as if her heart were spit, nothing of substance,
only a cold feeling.
And if I were to write poetry then
I would write prose—
Which is a difference in rhyme
and breath.

משהו פסיכי

הַאִם אַמְשִׁיךְ לִבְחֹשׁ בְּחוּשִׁים מַבְחִילִים?
חוֹדְרִים בֵּין סוֹרְגִים, מִתְקַפְּלִים אֶל הַחֲשֵׁכָה שֶׁבַּחֶדֶר
טַעֲמָם עֲרָפֶל

רָצִיתִי לְהַגִּיעַ לַגֵּיהִנּוֹם הַזֶּה;
נִגְזֶרֶת שֶׁל טֵרוּף
וּמַשֶּׁהוּ פְּסִיכִי.
נִדְמֶה שֶׁמְּנוֹרוֹת הָרְחוֹב מְנַקְּזוֹת תְּאוּרָתָן
אֶל צְלָלִיּוֹת חַיָּלִים מְצֻפִּים, מְבַקְּשִׁים
אֶת הוֹרָאָתוֹ; דְּמָיוֹת מֵחַיִּים מְשַׁעַמְמִים

וְאֵין חֶרֶף!
זֶה כְּמוֹ הִתְפָּרְדוּת אֵינְסוֹפִית
שׁוּב וָשׁוּב
הִתְבַּצְּעוּת שֶׁל לֵב שָׁלֵם וְהַזְּמַן לֹא עוֹבֵר
הוּא תָּקוּעַ! הוּא תָּקוּעַ!

70

Crazy Thing

Will I keep stirring up these revolting feelings?
They penetrate between the slats, fold into the darkness of the room,
tasting like fog

I wanted to reach this hell:
A cognate of madness
and something crazy.
It seems that the streetlamps drain their light
into the shadows of soldiers waiting
for an order. Characters in a boring life

and no winter!
Like an endless partition
repeating
the working of a full heart but time doesn't move—
It's stuck stuck stuck

תִּקְוֹתֶהָ

סִימָנֵי הַתִּקְוָה יִתְיַבְּשׁוּ
אֵיפֹה שֶׁהִשְׁפַּכְתָּ זֶרַע שָׂטָן
עַל שָׁדֶיהָ.

עֲבוּר מָה לָאִשָּׁה הַשִּׁגְרָה
וְהִיא רוֹצָה אוֹר.

Her Hope

The signs of hope will dry up
where you spilled devil seed
over her breasts.

What good is a routine for a woman
and she wants light.

שיר על עיר

הוּא לֹא פָּסַע עִם אִשָּׁה קְטַנָּה
נוֹאֶקֶת
בְּקוֹל קוֹנְכִית,
בִּטְנָהּ מְלֵאָה גַּרְגְּרִים.

מַשַּׁב רוּחַ דּוֹבֵב אֶת הָעֵצִים בַּשְּׂדֵרָה
וְהָאָדוֹן
לְעַלַּע מִלִּים מְהֻדָּקוֹת עַל עֵץ הַיְּהוֹשֻׁעַ
וְיִקְבֵי הַכְּרָמִים שֶׁל סַן-פְרַנְסִיסְקוֹ
הַבַּאצ'וֹ הַזֶּה, הַסִּיטִי לַייט הַזֶּה
שָׁם יוֹשְׁבִים מִתְרוֹמְמִים
לוֹגְמִים מְלַמְלְמְלִים
עוֹנְדִים פּוֹנְפּוֹנִים מִתַּחַת לָאַף.

A Poem About a City

He's out of step with the small woman
moaning
like a shell,
her belly full of grain.

A breeze draws the chatter from trees on the avenue
and the master
croaks crowded words about the Joshua Tree
and the vineyards of San Francisco
this Bacco, this City Light
Sitting there moving up
sipping this mumblemumble
fastening pom-poms under their noses.

הצוענים

פָּגַשְׁתִּי צוֹעֲנִי שֶׁלָּקַח אוֹתִי לַנָּהָר, לֶאֱכֹל דָּג
לִרְאוֹת יֶלֶד קוֹפֵץ מִגָּבוֹהַּ.
הִגִּישׁ לִי תְּאֵנָה שֶׁקָּטַף וּבָצַע וּמָרַח עַל שְׂפָתַי.
אֵיךְ יַעֲזֹב אֶת הָעֲיָרָה הַזּוֹ?
אֶת הַגֶּשֶׁר?

קְרוֹאָטִי זוֹעֵק עַל קֶבֶר "הַסֶּרְבִּים עֲיֵפִים,
הַסֶּרְבִּים עוֹד יָשׁוּבוּ".
מִמּוּל רַק גְּבָעוֹת, יַעַר בָּטוֹן מְחוֹרָר
וְאוּד.

הַשָּׁמַיִם פְּרוּשִׂים מִלְּפָנִים, מֵאָחוֹר אַנְדַּרְטָאוֹת.
יֵשׁ לְנַפֵּץ אוֹתָן אֲנִי קוֹרֵאת אֵלֶיךָ
עָלֵינוּ לִשְׂרֹף הַכֹּל.

מְקֻלָּל בְּשֵׁדִים
חֲסַר בַּיִת,
אַתָּה הָאָהוּב הָאֵינְסוֹפִי, הָאַחֲרוֹן.

Roma

I met a Roma who took me to the river to eat fish
and watch a kid high diving.
He handed me a fig he had picked and split and smeared
                              it across my lips.
How can one leave this village?
This bridge?

A Croatian man cries over a grave: "The Serbs are tired,
the Serbs will come back."
There are only hills ahead, a forest of riddled concrete,
and an ember.

The sky stretches forward, monuments are behind.
They have to be crushed I call out to you
We have to burn everything.

Demon cursed
Homeless
You are the eternal lover, the very last one.

מוֹנוּ

שׁוּם דָּבָר נִפְלָא וּמַתִּישׁ
אָקוּם לְצִדְּךָ לְלֹא מַטָּרָה.
בְּבְרֵאשִׁית הַטִּפְּשׁוּת—
אֶתְגַּלְגֵּל בַּטְּרָשִׁים, כְּמוֹ עֲסוּי גַּב בְּמוֹרַד תֵּל מְדֻשָּׁא.
פַּעַם, הַכֹּל הָיָה אַחֶרֶת;
הַשֶּׁמֶשׁ לְמָשָׁל
זָרְחָה לְמָחֳרַת הַלַּיְלָה.

Mono

Nothing brilliant and draining
I'll get up next to you without a plan.
In the beginning was the stupidity—
I'll roll in the rock outcrop, like a back massage on a grassy slope.
Everything was different once.
For instance, the sun
would shine the night after.

למה זה מושלם

אַתָּה שׁוֹכֵב מְטֻלָּא
מִתְלוֹנֵן
עַל כָּל הַנָּשִׁים שֶׁהֶחְלִיטוּ
לִלְבֹּשׁ שְׂמָלוֹת קְטַנּוֹת
לְיַד תֵּבָה
לְצַחְקֵק לָמָּה זֶה
מוּ
eee
לַם!!!!1

מִישֶׁהוּ הִדְלִיף
אֲנָשִׁים מְרַכְלִים. יֵשׁ סִכּוּי
שֶׁנַּסְפִּיק לָשׁוּב אֶל הַמְּיֻחָד
הָרְחוֹבוֹת מַפְגִּינִים
הָיִינוּ שֶׁמֶן זַיִת
בְּעֵינַי.
תּוֹרִיד אוֹתִי כָּאן—
רֶגֶל בְּתוֹךְ נוֹרְמָלִיּוּת—
גַּם אַתָּה תֵּדְעַךְ כָּךְ
לַמְרוֹת הַסְּעָדָה, הַשְּׁנִינוּת
וְכָל שֶׁנּוֹתַר.

Why This is Great

You rest, patched up
and complaining
about those women who pick
tiny dresses to wear
next to a casket
and giggle why this is so
gr
8
!!!1

Someone leaked—
people gossip. There's a chance
we'll stop going back to that special thing—
The streets are on strike
I thought
We were olive oil
Let me out here—
One foot in normalcy—
You'll also fade like that
despite the feast, the wit,
and all that's left.

הַבֶּכִי, הַנִּגּוּנָה שֶׁל תַּרְמִית
מְעִיקָה
בִּגְרוֹנְךָ.

אוּלַי נִשְׁאַר
עַל הַבָּר
עוֹד שָׁעָה סְתָמִית,
נִסְתּוֹבֵב בֵּין הַגַּלֶרְיוֹת. עַל הַמִּטָּה מְנַמְנֵם פִּיל
וּבַכִּיּוֹר, עֲרֵמַת כֵּלִים מִשִּׁלְשׁוֹם.

רָאִיתִי
שֶׁבָּרַחְתָּ בִּשְׁנָתְךָ
וְהָאַרְגָּזִים מְחַכִּים בַּמִּסְדְּרוֹן לְצַד הַמַּדִּים.
עִם הַלִּיפְּסְטִיק
כָּתַבְתִּי "שַׁקְרָן" בְּמֶרְכַּז הָרְאִי.

The crying, the sound of a scam
clenches
in your throat.

Maybe we'll stay
at the bar
one more hour.
We'll walk around the galleries. An elephant naps on the bed.
There's a two-day old pile of dishes in the sink.

I noticed
that you fled in your sleep
and the boxes wait in the hallway by your uniform.
And with this lipstick
I wrote LIAR across the mirror.

רגע

אֲנִי מְזַהֶמֶת אֶת עַצְמִי בַּהֹוֶה בִּלְבַד;
הָיִיתִי רוֹצָה לִהְיוֹת אַחֶרֶת;
מַנְדָּט מְנֻסָּח שֶׁל תַּרְבוּת,
הֶעְדֵּר חִבּוּטִים וְאַרְנָק

מָחָר יִזְרְקוּ הַצְּעִירִים הַתֵּל אֲבִיבַיִּים תַּפּוּחִים אֶל הַשָּׁמַיִם
וְיִרְאוּ אוֹתָם נוֹפְלִים.
אֵינֶנּוּ חוֹלְפִים כְּמוֹ שֶׁהָיִינוּ צְרִיכִים
הָלַכְנוּ וְצָעַקְנוּ
בְּכַעַס גָּדוֹל.

Just a Minute

I pollute myself only in the present;
I would like to be someone else:
A well-edited cultural mandate,
no fist fights and no purse.

Tomorrow the youth of Tel Aviv will throw apples at the sky
and watch them fall.
We didn't move on the way we should have.
We walked and screamed
so mad.

נַעַר נוּטֶּלָה

יֶלֶד מְדַוֵּשׁ בְּרַעַל
נָשִׁים סְמוּיוֹת מְצַפּוֹת לוֹ מֵעֵבֶר לַנָּהָר, קוֹלָן יְלָלָה.
הוּא
הוֹלֵךְ
מְפַקְפֵּק
הוֹלֵךְ בַּפַּאְרְק וְתוֹהֶה אֵיךְ קָשְׁרוּ, אֵיךְ סִמְּמוּ, אֵיךְ הִפְשִׁיטוּ, אֵיךְ רָחֲצוּ אֶת גּוּפוֹ.
אֵיךְ הֵם חָקְרוּ אֶת הַשֵּׁדִים שֶׁיָּצְאוּ מֵרֹאשׁוֹ, אֵיךְ הוּא הִבִּיט בַּחֹרֶף.
הוּא הוֹלֵךְ עַל אֶבֶן גַּבִּירוֹל
צָעִיר מְשֻׁבָּשׁ הוֹלֵךְ בַּכְּבִישׁ לְצַד כְּרָמִים, בְּתַרְמִילוֹ כִּכַּר לֶחֶם וְצִנְצֶנֶת נוּטֶּלָה
יָשֵׁן עַל סַפּוֹת זָרִים, מְסַפֵּר לָהֶם עַל הָרְדִיפוֹת. עַל הַקּוֹלוֹת וְהַצַּעֲצוּעִים.
הוּא הוֹלֵךְ מְשֻׁגָּע
סוּסֵי מִשְׁטָרָה מוּלוֹ
הֲמוֹנִים יוֹשְׁבִים עַל הַמִּדְרָכָה בְּצַמֶּרֶת קַפְּלָן בּוֹהִים בּוֹ בַּחֲזָרָה.

Nutella Boy

A kid pedals poison.
Women hiding watch him across the river, wailing.
He
moves
doubts
He goes into the park wondering how they tied, drugged, stripped,
and washed him.
How they inspected the demons that came out of his head, how he
stared at the winter.
He walks along Ibn Gabirol—
A damaged boy walking past the vineyards. In his bag there's a loaf
of bread and a jar of Nutella.
He sleeps on the sofas of strangers, tells them about the pursuit.
About the voices and the toys.
He goes crazy
Police horses face him
The crowd sits on the sidewalk at Kaplan Junction and looks back
at him.

מילאנו

הֵם דּוֹחֲפִים יָדַיִם אֶל תּוֹךְ הַקִּיר
קַרְטוֹן נִשְׁבָּר
וְעַמּוּד הַשִּׁדְרָה נָמֵס.
אִי אֶפְשָׁר לִישֹׁן
יְלָדִים,
הֵם בּוֹעֲטִים בִּמְהַגֵּר מְכֻנָּף עַל הַמִּדְרָכָה
בִּרְחוֹב פַּדוֹבָה יֵשׁ סִמְטָה מְכֹעֶרֶת
חֲרֵשָׁה שֶׁנִּשְׂרֶפֶת לְאַט.

Milan

They push their hands into the wall
A cardboard box breaks
And the spinal column melts
Can't sleep
Children
Are kicking a winged immigrant on the sidewalk
On Via Padova there's a dirty alleyway
A grove slowly burning.

למען התמימות

שַׁחַף וְשַׂעֲרָה תָּמִיד עוֹנוֹת חוֹלוֹת
בְּכוֹסָהּ
הִיא מַצִּיעָה מֵהַתַּרְעֶלֶת, כְּשׁוּף הַטְּרָלָהלָהלָה.
אֶחֱזוּ בּוֹ! עֲבוּרִי.
הַמֶּרֶד,
הוּא עֵירֹם.
נִיחוֹחַ אֵיקָלִיפְּטוּס וּמַרְוָה
זְרִיחַת הָאַשְׁפָּתּוֹת

אֶכְתֹּב עַל הֶעָלִים כִּי נִמְאֲסוּ הָאֲנָשִׁים

מִחוּץ לַחַלּוֹן, עֲלוֹת הָעֵץ מְמַסֶּכֶת אֶת הָרַעַשׁ
זָעָה תַּחַת הַשֶּׁמֶשׁ
כִּמְעַט הָרוּחַ וְאֵין הַסְּעָרָה.

לִמַּדְתְּ אוֹתִי לֶאֱחֹז בְּרִמּוֹנִים
טֶרֶם נְשִׁירָתָם
זְהִירוּת, הֵם מִתְפּוֹצְצִים אֶל הָרִצְפָּה.

שׁוּב נַעֲלוּ הַדְּלָתוֹת, לָקְחוּ הַנַּעֲלַיִם
הִשְׁאִירוּ שְׂרוֹכִים.
הַשִּׁיר הַזֶּה נִכְתַּב לְמַעַן
הַתְּמִימוּת.

For the Sake of Innocence

A seagull and hair always sickly seasons
in her cup
she serves the poison, a *tralalalala* spell.
Hold him! Do it for me.
Revolt—
He's naked.
A perfume of eucalyptus and sage
Dungrise.

I'll write on the leaves because people are sick and tired

Out the window, tree leaves screen the noise
sweat under the sun
almost wind but no storm.

You taught me how to hold pomegranates
before they fall
careful, they burst on the ground.

The doors are locked again, they took the shoes
and left the laces.
This poem is written for
the sake of innocence.

הַלְוַאי וְהָיִיתִי יְכוֹלָה לֶאֱהֹב אוֹתְךָ עַכְשָׁו
הַשָּׁמַיִם אֲפֹרִים וּשְׁנֵי צִפֳּרִים פָּרְשׂוּ מִכָּאן.
טַנְקִים
עוֹמְדִים דּוֹמְמִים בַּמִּדְבָּר.

בָּאוֹטוֹבּוּס
מֵאַבּוּ דִּיס,
מְשׁוֹרֵר זָקֵן תּוֹהֶה
אִם אִשְׁתּוֹ הַמֵּתָה הִיא
רַעְיָתוֹ הָאַחֲרוֹנָה.

I wish I could love you now
the sky is grey and two birds have taken off from here.
Tanks
are standing quietly in the desert.

On the bus
from Abu Dis,
an old poet wonders
if his dead wife is
his last one.

זוויות

נְמֹדֵד אֶת הַמֶּרְחָק כָּךְ הַיָּרֵחַ נוֹגֵעַ
בָּנוּ
זוֹ רַק סַפָּה
רַק דִּירָה
זֶה
רַק
מָסַךְ מַחְשֵׁב.
אָז נִשְׂרַט, דָּפַקְתָּ אֶגְרוֹף.
נִבְהֶה בַּצִּנּוֹרוֹת הַמִּתְפַּתְּלִים.

בּוֹא נִהְיֶה
מַקְסִימִים. בְּסִיּוּם כָּל זֶה, נִבְגֹּד בַּהַכֹּל
נְפַחֵד מִמִּי שֶׁנִּשְׁאַר, נְאַבֵּד אֶת זְכוּתֵנוּ בַּתַּרְבּוּת
נַחְסֹךְ אֶת הֶעָתִיד.
דַּי לָנוּ
הַזְּכוּת לִפְעֹל
יֵשׁ רַכּוּת
שֶׁעוֹד לֹא אִמַּצְנוּ.
גְּבוּרַת הַמַּחְשָׁבָה נִמְצֵאת
מֵעֵבֶר לֶעָנָן
הַמֵּתִים יְשֵׁנִים
בְּכָל
רֶגַע
הֵם דּוֹלְקִים.

Angles

We'll measure the distance
the way the moon touches us
It's just a sofa
Just an apartment
It's
just
a computer screen.
Then it scratched and you threw a punch.
We'll stare at the winding pipes.

Let's be
fantastic. At the end of this, we'll betray everything
We'll fear who's left, we'll lose our right to culture
We'll save the future
We're done
with the right to work
there's a tenderness
we haven't adopted yet.
The bravura of thought lies
beyond the cloud
the dead sleep
and every
moment
they gleam.

פני המעמד

הַכְּבִישִׁים מוּצָפִים בְּמַיִם, אֲנָשִׁים רָצִים בַּשְּׁלוּלִיּוֹת
נִכְנָסִים אֶל בֵּית הַקָּפֶה, מְמַלְמְלִים "אֵיזֶה קֹר".
יָדַיִם מַחְלִיפוֹת עִתּוֹנִים מֻכְתָּמִים
אֶת הַבֶּן אָדָם הַזֶּה רָאִינוּ אֶתְמוֹל
הוּא לֹא יָרִים אֶת הָרֹאשׁ כְּשֶׁיְּסַפֵּר לַמֶּלְצַר
עַל הַמָּצוֹד שֶׁלּוֹ אַחַר הַכֶּסֶף, לְשַׁנּוֹת אֶת פְּנֵי הַמַּעֲמָד.
דָּבָר לֹא מִשְׁתַּנֶּה
הַגֶּשֶׁם מֵסֵב אֶת הָאֹזֶן
אֲנָשִׁים עוֹמְדִים דּוֹמְמִים מוּל הָרְחוֹב
שׁוּם דָּבָר לֹא הֶגְיוֹנִי
הָיִינוּ אֲמוּרִים לִשְׁכַּב בַּמִּרְפֶּסֶת,
לְהִתְעוֹרֵר בָּאֲשָׁרָאמִים, לִרְקֹד בָּאִיִּים
לְשַׁחְרֵר אֶת עַזָּה וּלְנַעֵר אֶת הַהוֹרִים.

96

Status

The streets flood with water, people run through puddles
They enter the café, murmuring "it's so cold."
Hands are trading stained newspapers
We saw that man yesterday
He won't lift his head when he tells the waiter
About chasing money to change his status.
Nothing will change
The rain turns the ear
People stand quietly in front of the road
Nothing makes sense
We were supposed to lie on the balcony,
Wake up in ashrams, dance on islands
Liberate Gaza and shake up our parents.

שירת אריזה

בְּקַעֲרַת הָאָרֶץ בָּנָנוֹת לֹא בְּשֵׁלוֹת
קְלִפּוֹת וְזַרְעֵי קִיקָיוֹן יְבֵשִׁים בִּצְנִצֶנֶת
מִחוּץ לַחַלּוֹן נוֹצוֹת וּגְבָבָה
כָּךְ בּוֹלְשִׁים עֲדַיִן.

מַקְלוֹת הָאֹכֶל מֻנָּחִים בָּאֶלֶכְסוֹן
תּוֹאֲמִים אֶת תְּזוּזַת הָעוֹפוֹת לְאֹרֶךְ הַמַּפָּל
כֵּיצַד הֵם מַנִּיחִים לַתִּמְסֹרֶת וּמַמְשִׁיכִים לֶאֱכֹל אֹרֶז
לִקְרַאת הַנְּדִידָה הַלֵּילִית?
כִּסּוּי בְּצֵל מַחְשְׁבוֹת הַשָּׁוְא,
כָּל שֶׁרָצִיתִי הָיָה לְהַצְבִּיעַ וּלְהַזְהִיר "זוֹהִי מְגִדּוֹ"
לִשְׁאֹל אִם יֵשׁ לַזָּרִים
סִירוֹת מְגוּמִי.

וְהַפָּרְנוֹיוֹת, וְהַפָּרְנוֹיוֹת, אֵין דָּבָר בָּהֶן
מִלְּבַד עַמּוּד תְּלִיָּה
לְהַעֲמִיס עַל הַשְּׁרִירִים
לִמְשֹׁךְ אֶת הַגּוּף
בַּחֶדֶר הַכָּשֵׁר
אִשָּׁה שׁוֹכֶבֶת עֵירֻמָּה בְּסָאוּנָה, לוֹחֶשֶׁת רְכִילוּת
וְהַמַּחְשָׁבוֹת בּוֹרְחוֹת מִמֶּנָּה
יַחַד,
הֵן הַתְּרוּפוֹת עוֹבְדוֹת, הֵן הָרֹאשׁ דָּמוּם
וְלִפְעָמִים, כְּשֶׁמִּתְרַכְּזִים, שׁוֹמְעִים מָטוֹס נוֹחֵת

Packing Poem

In the rice bowl, green bananas
and peels, dry castor beans in a jar,
feathers and mulch outside the window
this is how they still gather evidence.

The chopsticks rest diagonally
matching the movement of birds along a waterfall.
How can they stall their transmission and keep eating rice
before their night migration?
Under the cover of delusions,
all I wanted was to point and warn everyone "that's Armageddon"
to ask whether foreigners have
inflatable boats.

And those paranoid, paranoid women have nothing
but the gallows
for overloading muscles
for stretching the body
in the gym
a woman lying naked in the sauna gossips under her breath
and the thoughts escape her
all at once
yes the meds work, yes the mind is numb
but sometimes, if you concentrate, you can hear an airplane landing

הדרך הזו

לְהַעֲבִיר לְבוֹדֶדֶת, לַחֲזֹר לְאֶחָז בַּמִּתְפָּס. יָד שְׁנִיָּה קְפוּאָה, אֶצְבַּע בִּשְׁמוּרַת הַהֶדֶק.
רִיצוֹת חַסְרוֹת מַשְׁמָעוּת מִסָּבִיב לְאֹהֶל
תֵּאַטְרוֹן בַּמִּדְבָּר.

נוֹסְעִים בַּכְּבִישׁ הַמָּהִיר לְצַד מְקָרְרִים עַל מַשָּׂאִית,
מְפַתְּחִים רְגָשׁוֹת
כְּלַפֵּי
הַדֶּרֶךְ הַזּוֹ
אֶל שְׂדֵה הַתְּעוּפָה.

This Way

Switch to semi-automatic, hold the clip again. The other hand frozen,
finger on the trigger.
Senseless running around the tent
Desert theater.

Driving in the fast lane next to a truckload of freezers,
developing feelings
for
this way
to the airport.

בפירינאים

יָשַׁבְנוּ בְּתוֹךְ בְּרֵכָה מְקֹרָה בַּפִּירֶנֶאִים, בּוֹהִים
בִּשְׁנֵי צַיָּדִים גּוֹרְרִים חֲזִירֵי בָּר בְּמוֹרְדוֹת הַשֶּׁלֶךְ
הִכַּרְתָּ אוֹתִי בְּלִי מַפָּה, עַל עֲקֵבִים, עִם שֵׂעָר מְסֹרָק
עִם הַהוּא שֶׁגַּרְתִּי אֶצְלוֹ וְהִרְעִיב
אֲנִי תָּמִיד גָּרָה עִם מִישֶׁהוּ
רְעֵבָה.

בָּעֶרֶב בַּשּׁוּק, לְמַרְגְּלוֹת מִנְזָר, מוֹכֵר הַצְּבִיעַ עַל מַרְכַּלְתּוֹ
בְּבָה מֻנַּחַת מִתַּחַת לִמְכוֹנִית צַעֲצוּעַ
"בֶּנְג בֶּנְג" קָרָא הָרוֹכֵל
אַחַר הִגִּישׁ לִי חֲלֵב פַּנְתֵּרוֹת
וְסִיָּרְנָה עָבְרָה
חָשַׁבְתִּי עַל חֲדַר הַמַּדְרֵגוֹת בְּתֵל אָבִיב, חִכִּיתִי לְפִיצוּץ הַפָאגֶ'ר
זֶה קוֹרֶה עַכְשָׁו
אֲנִי בֶּן אָדָם אַחֵר מֵאָז שַׂר הַמִּלְחָמָה שֶׁעָבַר.

In the Pyrenees

We sat in an indoor pool in the Pyrenees, staring
at two hunters dragging wild boars down autumn slopes
you met me without a map, with my high heels and combed hair
living with that guy who starved
I am always living with someone
and hungry.

In the evening at the market, at the foot of a monastery, a seller
                                pointed at his wares
a doll lying under a toy car
bang bang the peddler cried out
then offered me panther milk
and a siren passed by
I thought about that stairwell in Tel Aviv, waiting for the shock
                                of the Fajr
it's happening now
since the last Minister of War, I am someone else.

החובשים

זוֹ עֲצִימַת עַיִן אֲדִישָׁה
תְּנוּעָה אִטִּית מִזְרוֹעוֹת חוֹבְשֵׁי הַכּוֹבָעִים
הֵם מְבָרְכִים אוֹתוֹ. יֵשׁ אָדָם שֶׁמְּנַסֶּה לֶאֱחֹז וְלֹא מַסְפִּיק
עֹצֶם הָעַיִן חוֹלֵף עַל פְּנֵי הַחֲשֵׁכָה.
שִׂימוּ לֵב לַחֲלָלִים הָרֵיקִים.

The Hat Wearers

It's the closing of a lazy eye
The slow-motion arms of the hat wearers
They bless him—one man tries to hold on but not enough
The might of the eye passes over the darkness.
Pay attention to the empty spaces.

בזבוז

נָשִׁים מִתְנוֹדְדוֹת מִצַּד לְצַד, מְחַכּוֹת לַחֲלֹק
עֲצֵי לִימוֹן מַסְתִּירִים אֶת הַיָּמִים הָאֲרֻכִּים
וְנִשְׁאַר רַק
לִשְׁמֹעַ צִפֳּרִים
לְחַכּוֹת בַּתּוֹר לַטֶּלֶפוֹן הַצִּבּוּרִי
לְהַאֲמִין בְּבִטְחוֹן הַשָּׁעוֹת הַחוֹלְפוֹת
לִרְאוֹת אֶת הַבִּזְבּוּז,
בִּזְבּוּז הָעֶצֶב וְהַנְּשִׁימוֹת

לִפְעָמִים,
אֲנִי הוֹלֶכֶת בַּמִּסְדְּרוֹן וְרוֹאָה גְּבָרִים שֶׁרָצִיתִי
וְאֵין לִי מַה לוֹמַר לָהֶם.
אֲנַחְנוּ מְחַיְּכִים וְחוֹצִים אֶת הַדֶּרֶךְ.

Waste

Women wander from side to side, waiting to share
Lemon trees hide the long days
And all that's left
Is to listen to birds
To wait in line for the public phone
To believe in the security of passing hours
To see the waste
The waste of grief and breath

Sometimes
I walk through the hall and see men that I wanted
But I have nothing to say to them.
We smile and cross the street.

שיר עָרִים חוֹרְפִּי

בַּקּוֹמָה הַ-26,
בַּצָּפוֹן
שִׁכְבַת גֶּשֶׁם
מְכַסָּה אֶת הָרְצָלְיָה. מֵהַחַלּוֹן הַזֶּה, אֲנִי יְכוֹלָה לִרְאוֹת
גַּם אֶת חֹרֶף 2002. יֵשׁ רַעַשׁ שֶׁל סַעֲרַת גַּלִּים,
יֵשׁ רֵיחַ שֶׁל יָם צָהֹב
יֵשׁ קֹר וְלֹא מְשַׁנֶּה הָעִיר. אֲנִי נוֹסֶקֶת לְאַטְלָאט
לְבַדְלְבַד
עִם בְּדִיּוּק.

בְּבֵית הַקָּפֶה, לָחַשׁ לִי גֶּבֶר שֶׁיָּשַׁב מֵאֲחוֹרַי:
"אַתֶּם שְׁקוּעִים בַּשִּׂיחָה וְזֶה יָפֶה, נִדְמֶה שֶׁמַּשֶּׁהוּ שׁוֹנֶה מִכָּל הָעוֹלָם מִתְרַחֵשׁ פֹּה"
"זֶה רֶגַע הִיסְטוֹרִי," סִפַּרְתִּי לוֹ. "וְזֶה נִרְאֶה כָּךְ" הִנֵּהֶן וְהִדְחַקְתִּי אֶת כָּל הַלֵּילוֹת שֶׁלֹּא
הָיוּ, כִּי הֵן לֹא הָיוּ.

בְּאוֹר הַשֶּׁמֶשׁ, אָז בְּפָּרִיז;
הִתְחַבֵּאתִי בְּמֵיצָג צְדָדִי שֶׁל קוֹלְנוֹעַ רֵיק וְרָצִיתִי לְהִזְדַּיֵּן
שָׁם בַּמֶּרְכָּז פּוֹמְפִּידוּ, לְדַמְיֵן שֶׁעָשִׂיתִי אֶת זֶה,
בְּתוֹךְ הַבְּרֵכָה הַדַּקָּה הַמַּזְלִיפָה
שֶׁפְּרִיצִים אֶל גַּגּוֹת-הָעִיר
פָּ ר י זזז

אֲבָל כַּמּוּבָן שֶׁיָּרַד הַגֶּשֶׁם

Winter City Poem

On the 26th floor
up north
a sheet of rain
covers Herzliya. From this window, I can also see
the winter of 2002. Storm waves pounding,
there's a Yellow Sea smell,
it's cold and the city doesn't change. I am taking off *sloooow*
alonealone.
Exactly with.

In the café, a man sitting behind me whispered:
"You're deep in conversation and that's nice, like something out
                              of this world is happening here."
"It's an historic event," I told him. "Seems to be," he nodded, and
                              I repressed all those nights
that never happened, because they never did.

In the daylight, back in Paris
I vanished into the sideshow of an empty movie theater and
                              wanted to fuck someone
in the Centre Pompidou, to imagine that I had
in the shallow pool
spraying the city rooftops
Parissss
But of course, it rained.

וּבְדָה-לָאת, שָׁכַבְתִּי לְבַד עַל הַמִּטָּה הַגְּדוֹלָה, בָּאַכְסַנְיָה הַיָּפָה
בָּעֲיָרָה הַצִּיּוּרִית דַּה-לָאתֶת.
קָרָאתִי מָגָזִינִים בְּאַנְגְּלִית וְשָׁמַעְתִּי אֶת הַלְּבַדדה.

קְרִי הָאַהֲבָה הִיא לֹא הַחַיִּים,
אֶלָּא נִדְבָּךְ סְכָּה
עַל חֻלְצָה
שֶׁמְּסִירִים.

In Da Lat, I slept alone on a big bed, in a beautiful hostel,
in picturesque Da *Lat-t-t-t*.
I read magazines in English and heard *aloooooone*

e.g., love is not life
but a pin stuck
to a shirt
they pull off.

*

אֶל הַקֹּר הַחַד סְטְרֵי מְפַזֶּרֶת
גְּבָרִים נֶעֱלָמִים בַּחֹשֶׁךְ,
וְהָעִיר הַגְּדוֹלָה
מְנַצְנֶצֶת אוֹרוֹת נֵיאוֹן,
נְקֻדּוֹת חֲמוּצוֹת מְבַעְבְּעוֹת.

*

Into the one-way cold she scatters
Men vanishing in the dark
And the big city
Glitters neon lights
Bubbling sour dots.

עין הכמהין

אדם קם בבוקר בעיר אחת ומחליט לשנות זהות. הוא יהיה אישה היום;
שְׂעַר האישה רולדה עם קשקשים של פרג. מצחה גורד שחקים. פיה
מנורת ניאון. עיניה פטריות כמהין. ידיה פקוחות, מושטות בהיכון לאסוף
ולברך אנשים עוברים מולה על המדרכת. עתידה במה שהיא נוטלת
והחלטותיה מטרידות.

היא נשענת על עגלת קבצים. העגלה מתרחקת ממנה והיא נופלת.
אנשים בוהים בה מעבר לזכוכית, מחייכים בהתבַּיְשות וממשיכים
ללכת. היא אוספת את עצמה מהרצפה ונעמדת לגהץ את שמלתה,
מושכת את העגלה ומטייחת ומטנפת את מצחה; "העניינים לא יכולים
להמשיך כך", היא נאנחת וחוזרת אל הדלפק.

כך היום עובר ובדרך מקרה, נעלמה לאווה הראייה בעין אחת ונאלצה
לשרטט בלי לאמוד את הזוויות. יעקב יאמר לה שתפסיק להתעסק
בתוכנת המשרד ושתלך אל הקנבס, כי עין כזו עוד לא התגלתה. אווה
תשיב שתשקול זאת ולעת עתה תלך אל הרופא – שיבדוק הדוקטור את
כישוריה.

יצאה מן המשרד אל השדרה, לכיוון בניין הרפואה. בחוץ, יום שמש
יפה ואווה מחליטה שתשב על ספסל ותבהה קצת בכביש. תנסה לבחון
דברים על החולף מולה ואיך זה מתרשם עם עין עצומה אחת.
לידה, קהל גברים מעונב, עם כוסות קפה קר ביד, מתחילים ללחשש,
"זו היא? זו היא?" מתבלבלים.

The Truffle Eye

One morning a man wakes up in some city and decides to change his identity. Today he'll be a woman with hair like a poppy seed bun. A skyscraper forehead. A neon light mouth. A woman with truffle eyes. Her hands open and reach out to gather and bless the people walking by on the pavement. Her future is in this undertaking. But her decisions still plague her.

She leans on a file cart. It rolls away and she falls down. People stare at her through the window. They offer embarrassed smiles but keep walking. She picks herself up from the floor and tries to smooth her dress. She wipes and smudges her forehead. *Things can't go on like this*, she sighs and goes back to her desk.

The day goes by and then, unexpectedly, Eva goes blind in one eye but has to keep drawing without properly gauging the angles. Jacob tells her to stop messing with the software and to go back to the drawing board, because an eye like hers is a real find. Eva says that she'll think about it. Meanwhile, she'll go to the doctor so he can assess her skills. She walks out of the office and into the avenue, toward the doctor's office. The sky is clear and Eva decides that she'll sit on a bench and watch the road. She'll try to examine every passerby in detail and see what kind of impression this makes with one closed eye.

שמועה זו הביאה להתעוררות זכרים רבים. התאספו כולם בצומת המרכזית וצהלו; הם תיארו קווי מתאר והגו תוכניות פעולה. העיר נתנה לה דממה זמנית לקראת מלחמת התורה החילונית. ובבוא הערב, עדר מעלי גירה ביצעו את הלוחות וצעדו אל ביתה עם שלטים ומקלות ופרחים. שירים כתובים על מצחם בדם. נהמו, "אנחנו כאן! אנחנו כאן!" החלו מתדפקים מזיעים ומטונפים על דלתות ומרעידים חלונות.

אווה שבה מבניין הרפואה כשהיא אוחזת בניירת תוצאות בדיקות ובשקית של סמים. חלפה על יעקב, שנשען בבטחה על עגלת הקבצים. חייך אליה ונופף בידו בחביבות. הפריח לעברה נשיקות ועיניו רומנטיות הלאה לאיפה שם, רחוק. אחר התאושש והמשיך לנופף לשאר העוברים.

מול ביתה, היא מביטה בסערה האנושית שנקרתה. היא הודפת ופורסת את דרכה אל הפנים. אווה נמשכת אחורה באלימות, שמלתה נקרעת, שערה מתפזר מפקעתו, גרגירים נופלים מראשה. אווה ממהרת לסגור את הדלת ולהישען עליה באימה. בחוץ, רעשים עדיין. לחנים מתנגנים והביאו גם תופים ושאר תגבורת.

"תפתחי", הם זועפים ורועמים. "את מעניינת", קוראים. במקום לציית, צנחה אווה עירומה אל המיטה וסתמה את פיה ואטמה את אוזניה. היא מסממת את החלל שלא שומעת בקללות אובדניות על פגרה ובצורת. "העניינים לא יכולים להמשיך כך", מחליטה והתרוממה בכל זאת. מביטה אל מעבר לחלון, פרצופים מתועבים מרוחים על הזכוכית, בוהים בה, החשופה. אווה מתעלמת ממבטם המפליל והוזה כרי ערוגות דשא ממחוזות הזיכרון של יעקב. ופה המקום לספר ששני ילדים מטופשים וחסרי משמעות, עם עיניים הפכפכות, עם הגב אל הקהל, כחכחו בגרונם והחלו יורקים הרחק באומץ אל המכוניות שעל הכביש. "אדם החליף זהות! החליף זהות!" השתעשעו הילדים ברכילות. מבטיחים לעצמם הפרחים, שכשהם יהיו גדולים – הם יהיו עשירים ומפורסמים מאוד.

A group of necktied men holding cups of cold coffee gather next to her. They hiss, *Is she the one? Is that her?* They are baffled. The rumor arouses more men. They congregate at the main intersection and revel; they outline her curves and devise plans of action. The city gives her a brief respite before this secular biblical war. But by evening, a herd of beasts has come to her house bearing signs, sticks and flowers. Poems written in blood on their foreheads. They growl, *We're here! We're here!* Sweaty and filthy, they begin to knock on the doors and rattle the windows.

Eva leaves the doctor's office gripping her lab results and a bag of medicine. She passes Jacob, who leans too trustingly against the file cart. He smiles and gives her a friendly wave. He blows her kisses with his aloof romantic eyes. Later he snaps out of it and goes on waving to the passersby.

In front of her house, she sees a human storm gathering. Eva deflects it and cuts a path inside. But she is dragged back violently, her dress torn, her bun unwinding, seeds falling from her head. She hurries to close the door and leans against it, terrified. Outside, the noises continue. Musicians jam together and bring drums and reinforcements.

Open up, they thunder. *You're interesting!* they scream. Instead of complying, Eva falls naked onto her bed, shuts her mouth and covers her ears. She drugs her space to block out their suicidal raving. *Things can't go on like this*, she decides and gets up anyway. She looks out the window, at the deplorable faces smeared against the glass, seeing her stripped bare. Eva overlooks their incriminating

אווה שולפת את העין המקולקלת שלה ומניחה אותה על אדן החלון,
שתצפה על המופרעים. הביטו הזכרים בעין המרתקת, ריר בשפתיהם
והם מכריזים מחירים על העין הזו. צועקים, "תפתחי. תפתחי. נקנה ממך
את העין הזו". אווה נדרכת מהעניין ושבה לפקוח את החלון.
כולם בחוץ, צועדים לאחור ביראה.

"טוב, אבל העין הטובה נשארת אצלי", מכריזה ברוב משמעות וידיה
על מותניה בקשיחות. צווארה מתעבה. מעבר לשקט שהשתרר
בהצהרתה הזו, הבליח קולו של אחד – ידוען של המקום; במאי,
תסריטאי, משורר, עיתונאי, עורך, שחקן, זמר, דוגמן, "אבל גם את העין
ההיא שלך", קרא הלה והחל צועד לכיוונה בהתברוזווזות, מנופף בשטרות
ובחוזים. עיניו זוהרות וגופו בריא והוא מדופלם בגינוני ההתנשאות.
השאר מריעים לו ומתכופפים לפניו. "שייקחו הם את הרקובה, אני
רוצה את זאת", מצביע בהחלטיות אל עין הכמהין שנותרה בביתה. הוא
מושיט ידו בתשוקה, לחטוף ממנה את שלה והיא נבהלת וסוטרת לו.
"ג'נטלמן", נובחת והקהל משתולל מהנאה וצוחק אל המחזה. "זו העין,
עדיין בריאה בגופה", מבארת לו. "שום כסף לא ייקח ממני את המיטב
שבי", ומגרדת בראשה, קלחת במצחה ופרג צומח מחדש על חוטמה.
כאן הוא מהסס. האחד הידוען (במאי, תסריטאי וגו') מהרהר ושולף
הצעה חדשה, "תני לי אותה ואעשה אותך דמות ידועה בציבור, תהיי
עיקרית אצלי. אתעסק רק בך, לא תהיי פרובינציאלית יותר."

אווה מתרגשת, ואין אלה הקישוטים החיצוניים והגינונים אצלו, אלא
נדמה שבאמת הרגישה בשורה אחרת במילותיו. ניגשת אל הדלת ורואה
את כולם כבר עוטים אל המבצר, זורמים אליה במהירות והיא מסננת,
"פנימה! נו, כנס כבר!" והוא נכנס יחיד אל מפתנה.

gaze, hallucinating the grassy meadows of Zichron Yaakov. And here's where you should know that two stupid, useless kids with fickle eyes turned away from the crowd, cleared their throats and bravely spit at the cars on the road. *This man changed his identity! This man changed his identity!* the boys tattled with glee. And the punks promise each other that when they grow up they will be really rich and famous.

Eva pulls out her rotten eye and places it outside on the window-sill so it can observe these psychopaths. The men look at her intriguing eye and drool their price. *Open up. Open up,* they shout. *We'll buy that eye from you.* This piques Eva's interest and she goes back to open the window.

Everyone steps back in awe.

Ok, but the good eye stays with me, she says and puts her hands on her hips. Her throat tightens. Beyond the silence that prevails after her announcement, a voice flares—the local (director, screenwriter, poet, journalist, editor, actor, singer, model) celebrity. *But that eye is also yours,* he says and waddles toward her waving bills and contracts. His eyes shine; his body is healthy; he is certified in the etiquette of arrogance.

The rest of them cheer him on and bow before him. *You guys can have the rotten one, I want that one,* he points decisively at the truffle eye that remains inside the house. He holds out a covetous hand to snatch away what is hers, but she slaps him away in horror. *Gentlemen,* she barks, and the audience, wild with pleasure, laughs

"יפה", אומרת משולהבת וסוגרת את הדלת, "ואני ילידת העיר, לא פרובינציאלית ממילא", ממשיכה. הולכת להחליף בושם על עצמה; "פשוט לתלוש את זה ולהגיש לך כך סתם? כך סתם?" שואלת באופן מרושע.

האחד הידוען, מסרק את שערו הסתור על עיניו ומשפשף את מבטו הזוהר. "לעקור את שלי ואשים את שלך במקום זה", אומר מחושב. הוא ניגש אל המטבח מחטט במגירות, שולף כפית קינוח ומתחיל חופר בעיניו. "בחיים לא הרגשתי כך", אומר נלהב ושוקק. כשגלגל עינו הזוהר יוצא מהחור ומדלג אל ספל הקפה שעל השיש, הוא מושיט אליה את ידו, "תני לי. תורך". אווה עושה כמותו וכעת היא עיוורת, מגישה לו את מאורה, "לפחות אני מריחה טוב", מכריזה נכה.
ברגע שהתקין האחד הידוען, את עין הכמהין אצלו, הבחין בראשו – איך זה נלחץ ולאט לאט מצטמצם אל תוך מרכז פניו.
אווה לדידה, נזכרה ששקית הסמים שלה על הרצפה ברחוב, לצד קרעי התלבושת שלה. מיהרה אל כיוון הדלת, מגששת את הדרך. בעילגות היא פותחת את החלון וקוראת אל הגברים שבחוץ, "הסמים שלי. תחפשו לי. תביאו לי. אני לא רואה כלום". וההם מתכופפים לארוך את חפציה הפזורים ומגישים לה. הם גם מנצלים את ההזדמנות לגעת בשדה ונוגעים בשאר גופה. אווה חוטפת וסוגרת את החלון, נועלת את התריסים ומתרווחת. בולעת מהר את הכדורים.
"כואב לי הראש," אומר האחד הידוען ואוחז בראשו; מרגיש שנעלם עוד רגע. "אני גם לא רואה כל כך טוב. נדמה לי שאת גבר", הבחין בה מטושטשת והיא שרועה על הרצפה, מושיטה ידה שוב אל אדן החלון. חופנת את העין המקולקלת ומגישה אל פיה בתאווה. "מה עוד?" שואלת בהתחסדות. הוא איננו יציב, רועד ונופל לצדה.

at the spectacle. *The eye in this body is still viable,* she explains to him, *no amount of money can take the best of me.* And scratching her head, her brow boils and a poppy grows back on her nose. Now he hesitates. The (director, screenwriter, etc.) celebrity thinks about it and makes a new offer. *Give it to me, you small town thing, and I'll make you famous. You'll be my girl.*

Eva's getting excited, and not because of his charms and mannerisms, but because she feels that his words really do convey different tidings. She approaches the door and sees everyone swooping in for the siege. *Inside! Come on,* she mutters. *Get in—now!* and he crosses the doorstep alone.

Fantastic, she says ecstatically and closes the door. *By the way, I'm no small town girl. I was born here—in this city,* she adds. She goes to put on some perfume. *So, I'll just rip it out and give it to you just like that, huh? Just like that?* she asks wickedly.

The celebrity combs back the hair covering his eyes and rubs his shining gaze. *I'll rip mine out and put yours in its place,* he says calculatingly. He goes into the kitchen and rummages through the drawers, pulls out a dessert spoon and starts to gouge out his eyes. *I've never felt anything like this,* he chirps. His shining eye comes out of the hole and bounces toward the coffee mug on the marble top. He holds his hand out to her. *It's your turn.* Eva does as he did and now she's blind. She hands over her vision. Disabled now, she declares: *At least, I smell good.*

"המוח שלי כמו רחת לוקוס", הוא ממלמל שיכור בעוד אווה נוגסת בכמהין. "נפלא. נפלא. תספר לי עוד", והבטיחה שעוד רגע תאכל לו את המוח .המתוק.

"ואם יש בך אהבה להעניק לי——" כעת היא מבקשת בפלרטוט את ספל הקפה שעל השיש, וניאות להביא לה.

היא מגששת על הרצפה ורוצה לגעת בו. גוררת את גופה אליו. "הכדורים מתחילים להשפיע עליי", חשה בדמותו הרוכנת אליה וספל קפה ביניהם. אווה לוגמת מן הנוזל החם ולועסת לו את העין. "נשוחח על היקום", היא לוחשת ובפיה הבל הקפאין. "תתקרב אליי", מתבטלת והוא משתנק ורופס, רוצה לגעת בה ונתקל בספל ונשפך.

"איך קוראים לך? בת כמה את? מאיפה את?" הוא שואל. הוא מדבר על אהבה. הוא מבולבל, הוא נכלולי והכול משתנה בו. הוא מאבד צלילות ומסיח את דעתו, נמשך אל הריח. "אני מכאן", היא לוחשת והם מתעלסים בגרגרנות איומה ומתהפכים ומשתנים. משרטטים דברים של עכשיו. "מהעיר הזו", משיבה שוב מתייגעת. ראשם קל על גופם, "אני אוהבת את העיר הזו". בחוץ, שריקות ותפילות בינתיים. ההם שולפים עמדות, בהיכון מתכוונים. הפרחחים המטופשים חסרי המשמעות, בולעים את הרוק. "כעת, הוא אדם שוב! חו חוה!" הם מציצים וקובעים. מאחורי גבם, פקק מכוניות אטי ויציב.

בסוף הכביש הארוך, ארובת רדינג.

After adjusting the truffle eye, the celebrity notices his head, how it is compressed and shrinking bit by bit into the center of his face.

Then Eva remembers the drugs sitting on the street, next to her shredded outfit. She hurries to the door, feeling her way. She opens the window clumsily and calls out to the men outside, *My pills. Look around and bring them to me. I can't see a thing.* And they bend over to gather the scattered objects and hand them to her. They also seize the opportunity to grab her breast and touch the rest of her body. Eva snatches the bag and closes the window, shuts the blinds and puts her feet up. She quickly swallows the pills.

My head hurts, the celebrity says, holding his head. He feels like he'll disappear any second now. *I can't see very well. From here you look like a man.* He sees her through a blur, flat on the floor, once more extending her hand to the windowsill. Cupping the rotten eye, she brings it to her ravenous mouth. *What else?* she asks sanctimoniously. He loses his balance, shakes and falls to the floor next to her.

My head is like a Turkish delight, he mumbles in a stupor while Eva nibbles on the truffle. Lovely. Lovely. *Tell me more,* she says and promises that next she'll eat his sweet head.

If you still love me . . . she says and points flirtatiously to the coffee mug on the marble top. He consents.

She gropes around the floor and wants to touch him. She drags her body to him. *The pills are starting to work,* she whispers to the body leaning toward her, the coffee mug still between them. Eva sips from the hot liquid and chews his eye. *Let's talk about the universe*, she whispers releasing coffee vapor. *Come closer*, she says languidly, and he gags and goes limp. He wants to touch her, but his fingers find the mug and it tips over.

What's your name? How old are you? Where are you from? he asks her. He talks about love. He's puzzled, but devious, and everything changes inside of him. No longer lucid, distracted, he's pulled toward the scent. *I'm from here*, she whispers, and they have furious, greedy sex, turning over and over and changing. They sketch current things. *From this city*, she replies, their weary heads fall lightly against their bodies. *I love this city*. In the meantime, the whistles and prayers make their way in. They draw their positions, standing at the ready. Those stupid, useless punks swallow their spit. They peek in and declare: *He's become a man again! And that's his Eve!* Behind them, traffic moves, slow and steady.

At the end of the long road—the Reading power station.

Notes

Mekong River: When I read this translation at a conference on diasporic Hebrew literature at the University of Cambridge, my colleagues insisted that the poem contains an allusion to Saint-Exupéry's *The Little Prince* ("draw me a sheep") and that I should change my "sketch" to "draw" (Vaan Nguyen was there as well and didn't disagree.). A few years later, I read this poem at an event at the University of Oxford, and several members of the audience insisted that I go back to "sketch," a more violent verb. I have gone with the latter but include this note to acknowledge the allusion. *Ha-nasikh ha-katan* (The Little Prince) is also a popular bookstore in Tel Aviv.

Chaos: In Hebrew, *Maayan*, the name of the journal in which Nguyen's poetry debuted, means "fountain" and "source" in Hebrew.

Tell: The original Hebrew title, "Tel milim" (hill of words), rhymes with "Tel Aviv."

Jaffa D: "Jaffa Dalet," a neighborhood in south Jaffa, is also known as "Givat ha-temarim" (Fig Hill). Built in the 1970s, it consists mostly of tenements. The word "dalet" is the fourth letter of the Hebrew alphabet.

Maayan: This poem quotes the famous line from François Villon's fifteenth-century poem "Ballade des dames du temps jadis" (Ballad of the Ladies of Times Gone By): "Mais où sont les neiges d'antan." My translation borrows from Dante Gabriel Rosetti's translation of the poem. The Hebrew includes Nguyen's own translation. See the note for "Chaos."

Metropolitan Pieces: The singer Mary Ocher set this to music under the title "Metropolitan Chapters" (Her recording is available on YouTube.). Her lyrics convinced me to change my translation "give up" to "leave."

Remembering Your Member: The Hebrew title "zokheret zakhrutkha" is a play on the homophonic relation between "memory" and "manhood" in Hebrew.

Orchid: Florentin is a trendy, bohemian neighborhood in south Tel Aviv.

Manhattan: The final line of the poem "ribat sha'atnez" translates literally as "a shatnez jam." In Hebrew, "sha'atnez" refers to cloth that contains both wool and cotton, a combination that is forbidden by Jewish law (see Leviticus 19:19 and Deuteronomy 22:11). In Modern Hebrew, it refers to a mixture or combination of disparate parts.

Jewish Boy: Ad Halom ("this far," "hitherto") is a bridge located at the eastern entrance to the city of Ashdod, south of Tel Aviv, and marks the northernmost point reached by the Egyptian army in one of the pivotal battles of the 1948 Arab-Israeli War. The expression appears in 2 Samuel 7:18, where God promises David a permanent dwelling. Today, Ad Halom junction is infamous for its traffic jams. For another version of this poem, and its first stanza in particular, see Lisa Katz's translation in *Poetry International* (https://www.poetryinternational.org/pi/poem/29658).

Highway 1: I first read the title as a reference to US 1, the highway that travels the full length of the United States East Coast. There is also a Highway 1 in Israel, which connects Tel Aviv and Jerusalem. According to Nguyen, it actually refers to the trans-Vietnam highway, National Route 1A (Quốc lộ 1A), which runs the length of the country. The line "a place and a name" comes from Isaiah 56:5. I have used the King James translation but Robert Alter renders this as "a marker and a name." The Hebrew, *yad va-shem*, is also the name given to the Holocaust museum in Jerusalem. Although *yad* is more commonly associated with "hand," in Hebrew it also refers to a monument or memorial, as well as to the pointer used for reading the Torah scroll.

The Last Landscape: LaGuardia refers here to a major thoroughfare in south Tel Aviv named after New York City mayor Fiorello La Guardia.

Why This is Great: I changed the Hebrew "perfect" (מושלם) to "great/gr8" in order to recreate the slang that appears in the first stanza of the poem.

In the Pyrenees: The line "the shock of the Fajr" refers to a long-range multiple launch rocket system developed in Iran and exported throughout the Middle East.

Winter City Poem: This and the short poem that follows were not published in *The Truffle Eye*. This version appeared several years ago on *Maayan*'s website, though those pages are now offline. A second version appeared online in *Maariv* (March 31, 2006). The major difference between the two versions concerns the first line of the last stanza. In the second version, the line translates as "the sound [*tslil*] of love that is not life." I have kept the earlier version with Nguyen's permission.

The Truffle Eye: Tel Aviv's Reading (רדינג) power station is a thermal power station located in the northwest corner of the city, near the mouth of the Yarkon River. It was built in 1938 during the British Mandate period and named after Rufus Daniel Isaacs, 1st Marquess of Reading.

Acknowledgments

I am grateful to PEN America for awarding me a 2015 PEN/ Heim Translation Grant, which supported the translation of this book. *Toda raba* to Lisa Katz, Evyn Lê Espiritu Gandhi, Yosefa Raz, Marcela Sulak, and Eran Tzelgov for their feedback and comments on this manuscript, and to Leora Zeitlin for her meticulous editing of the final draft. I also wish to thank Lihi Turjeman for giving us permission to use her work for the cover, one of seven diptychs from her series "The Atlas" (www.lihi-turjeman.com).

And the biggest thank you of all to Vaan Nguyen for trusting me with her poems and patiently answering my many questions over the years.

Earlier versions of these translations appeared in the following publications, in some cases under different titles:

"Mekong River," *Gulf Coast Review*, Vol. 27, No. 2 (Summer/Fall 2015): 56–57.

"Packing Poem," *Shofar: An Interdisciplinary Journal of Jewish Studies* 33.4 (Summer 2015): 103–104.

"Three Snapshots of Paris," "Loop," "*," *PEN America* (October 2015, online).

"Culture Stain" and "Tell," *Drunken Boat* #23 (Spring 2016, online) and *Poetry International* (2019, online).

"Packing Poem" and "Mekong River," *Inheriting the War: Poetry and Prose by Descendants of Vietnam Veterans and Refugees*, edited by Laren McClung (NY: W. W. Norton, 2017): 238–240.

"Metropolitan Pieces," *The Ilanot Review* (Summer 2017, online).

"Chaos," "For the Sake of Innocence," and "In the Pyrenees," *Seedings* #5 (2018, online).

Bios

Vaan Nguyen is the author of the poetry collections *The Truffle Eye* (Maayan Press, 2013) and *Vain Ratio* (Barchash, 2018). In addition to poetry, she has worked as an actress, journalist, and social activist. Translations of her poems have appeared in English and French, including in the collection *Inheriting the War: Poetry and Prose by Descendants of Vietnam Veterans and Refugees* (W. W. Norton, 2017). She currently lives in Jaffa, Israel, and is writing her first novel.

Adriana X. Jacobs is the author of *Strange Cocktail: Translation and the Making of Modern Hebrew Poetry* (University of Michigan Press, 2018). Her translations have appeared in various print and online journals, including *Gulf Coast, Seedings, World Literature Today, Poetry International, The Ilanot Review,* and the collection *Women's Hebrew Poetry on American Shores: Poems by Anne Kleiman and Annabelle Farmelant* (Wayne State UP, 2016). She is Associate Professor of Modern Hebrew Literature at the University of Oxford.